THE
BENEVOLENT
DICTATOR

THE
BENEVOLENT
DICTATOR

EMPOWER YOUR EMPLOYEES, BUILD YOUR BUSINESS, AND OUTWIT THE COMPETITION

MICHAEL FEUER
WITH DUSTIN S. KLEIN

WILEY

John Wiley & Sons, Inc.

Published by John Wiley & Sons, Inc., Hoboken, New Jersey.
Published simultaneously in Canada.

For general information on our other products and services or for technical support, please contact our Customer Care Department within the United States at (800) 762-2974, outside the United States at (317) 572-3993 or fax (317) 572-4002.

Wiley also publishes its books in a variety of electronic formats. Some content that appears in print may not be available in electronic books. For more information about Wiley products, visit our web site at www.wiley.com.

Library of Congress Cataloging-in-Publication Data:
Feuer, Michael
  The benevolent dictator: empower your employees, build your business, and outwit the competition/Michael Feuer.
     p. cm.
  ISBN 978-1-118-00391-6 (hardback)
  ISBN 978-1-118-06152-7 (ebk)
  ISBN 978-1-118-06153-4 (ebk)
  ISBN 978-1-118-06154-1 (ebk)
    1. New business enterprises—Management. 2. Entrepreneurship. I. Title.
  HD62.5.F493 2011
  658—dc22
                                                                2010050405

Printed in the United States of America
10 9 8 7 6 5 4 3 2 1

Contents

Phase Three   Constant Reinvention   107

Author's Note

"We don't need no more stinkin' business books."

The above is my version of the famous, frequently misquoted, and oft-parodied line from the movie *The Treasure of the Sierra Madre*. It is uttered by the Mexican bandit leader, played by Alfonso Bedoya, after Humphrey Bogart's Fred C. Dobbs challenges him by demanding, "If you're the police, where are your badges?"

Disgusted, Bedoya scoffs, "Badges? We ain't got no badges. We don't need no badges! I don't have to show you any stinkin' badges."

Drop the word "badges" and substitute the words "business books"—and this statement says it all. The world doesn't need another business book. But there is a need for a hands-on digest that uses proven street-fighter methods to build a business from scratch, create significant value, and help entrepreneurs figure out what it takes not just to survive, but to excel. To achieve these lofty and elusive objectives, *The Benevolent Dictator* focuses on lessons that will help you to build your business, empower your employees, and outwit your competition.

I have written this book with my long-time editor, Dustin S. Klein, of the management journal *Smart Business*. After producing more than seven years of monthly columns for *Smart Business*—which is published in 17 markets nationwide and read by more than 750,000 monthly readers—I finally decided that perhaps others could benefit from what I've experienced during my career of building businesses from the ground up.

And I've certainly read my share of business books over the years. Some were great, some were okay, and some really were stinkin'.

For that reason, I have steered clear of the theoretical, sophisticated hypothesis of what "should" work in this book. Instead, I've written a narrative of what has worked for me well beyond my wildest dreams—tactics that have returned millions to me during a time when my most fervent hope was sheer survival. Punctuated throughout are real-life experiences that enabled me to launch OfficeMax and grow it into a more-than-1,000-store international retail chain, followed by several other ventures, and now a new business, Max-Wellness, a first-of-its-kind health-and-wellness chain. With each of these undertakings, I had my share of both the thrills of victory and probably too many agonies of defeat—albeit none of which proved anywhere near fatal.

My aim in writing *The Benevolent Dictator* was to essentially create a road map for executives, managers, and want-to-be entrepreneurs. Is this real-life, how-to guide for absolutely everyone? Probably not. Can everyone at least learn something from the lessons and examples in this book? I certainly think so.

I've tried to explain throughout these pages how I got started, why I did it, and where I wound up, at least with OfficeMax. True confession: When you read this book, you'll realize—as

I have—that I've been incredibly lucky. However, I also hope that you'll recognize that people do indeed make their own luck—and that the real skill lies in being smart enough to recognize when luck is staring you in the face, and then seizing the opportunity when it's presented.

I'm also a self-confessed shameless promoter—and proud of it. I've always felt that it's a lot like flirting: If you do it in the dark and your intended recipient doesn't see you, you're really not flirting. Over the years, I have fine-tuned my own style of turning the lights on in that proverbial dark room and shining the spotlight on my undertakings. You'll find examples of that creative marketing sprinkled throughout the following pages as well.

My venture with OfficeMax allowed me to start with almost no money and build a $5 billion company in a relatively short period of time. This book tells you how I did it, the obstacles I encountered, and how I dramatically exceeded expectations for my team, investors, customers, and myself. By no measure were all of the times rosy. But I quickly learned how to stay off the rocks and, when I did hit them, how to extricate myself quickly and with as little damage as possible—even occasionally turning negatives into positives.

I had a number of "aha" moments while writing *The Benevolent Dictator*. I realized that it's just as important to learn from mistakes as from successes during one's career. It didn't take me long in my first job to recognize how much wasted time, energy, and money go into analyzing stuff about which a reasonable person would simply say, "Who cares?" This is because businesses are really no better off from the effort expended if they don't accrue tangible benefits for the customer, investors, or employees. On the flip side, too many projects never get off the ground because of a lack of creativity or determination. What really frustrates me is how many good things never make it off the drawing board because a management sponsor determines that there isn't anything "in it" for him or her.

As I wrote this book, I recalled the many hundreds and hundreds of lessons I learned during the earlier stages of my career, and constantly in the back of my mind I wondered, "What if I could do it my way?" I don't think I gave this truly serious thought during my early years; only later did I crystallize the concepts that I could employ in my next life, starting with OfficeMax. It's a lot like going on a vacation and not really understanding the positives of what you're experiencing while you're traveling about. It's usually not until a month or two later when you think back on that trip and recognize, "Damn, that was great." The same phenomenon occurred with the lessons to which I was exposed while I was just trying to get a job done. The ones I cover in this book that stand out most in my mind are:

- If you don't ask, you'll never get. This applies to vendors, employees, and even bosses.
- The word "no" is just a synonym for "maybe." This realization led me to train my team to comprehend that the "no" you receive the first nine times is merely a disguised "maybe"— because the other guy is looking for a reason why not to proceed, or doesn't understand what you're asking. It's only after the tenth time—when the other person hangs up on you or walks out of the room and slams the door—that "no" really means "no."
- You must always look at a new idea through the customer's eyes—not just from an operator's perspective.
- The journey had better be as much fun as the destination.

- Always play by the "Mother Rule": if you don't want your mother to know you did something, don't do it—because it is probably wrong.
- Never fall in love with the underpinnings of your idea. Instead, fall in love with the expected results that you might achieve. To put it more crudely, "Don't drink your own bathwater."
- Know when enough is enough and it's time to pull the plug on the project and pack it in.
- Know how to put lightning back in the bottle again and again.
- Understand why the best start-ups are run by a benevolent dictator.

I would take great pleasure and will have realized my goal in writing this book by knowing that readers obtained just one idea that they could translate into a successful reality in their own world. I would be ecstatic if a young entrepreneur read this book and used it in some small way to take his or her company to new heights. I would be absolutely thrilled if I provided the impetus to a dreamer to stop dreaming about starting a business—and just do it.

It's been said many times that imitation is the greatest form of flattery. Nothing would be more satisfying to me than if a reader created the next OfficeMax, starting as I did with my severe birth defect—poverty. In order to do so, however, the reader must start by understanding the four key business phases, which I've outlined in four distinct sections:

1. Start-up
2. Build out and put the idea to the test
3. Constant reinvention
4. The payday

I invite you to take from this book whatever is applicable to your needs and improve on what I did and the way I did it. I hope that along the way, you'll find it entertaining, a bit iconoclastic, and, most of all, useful. I learned a long time ago that one is allowed to do just about anything except bore an audience in writing, speaking, or actions.

And if this book helps me to create a new breed of benevolent dictators, then that will put a "W" on my personal scoreboard.

THE
BENEVOLENT
DICTATOR

Phase One

Start-Up

1

Lesson #1:
To Successfully Launch a Start-Up, There Must Be a Benevolent Dictator

THE TERM "DICTATOR" conjures up thoughts of the world's most despicable evildoers, from Idi Amin to Saddam Hussein, and many even worse. However, this designation is not always a pejorative when combined with the modifier "benevolent." In fact, the case could be made that being a *benevolent* dictator can make the difference when starting a business from scratch and with a scarcity of time and money.

Entrepreneurs fantasize, ponder, and calculate how to come up with that next big idea and translate it into fame and fortune, thereby fulfilling their own version of the American Dream. However, more often than not, people spend too much time dreaming and not enough time doing. The difference between success and failure is often simply a matter of getting started, fleshing out an idea, and then creating the building blocks to get from point A to point B—and from point B all the way to Z.

Doing this is certainly easier said than done. As business history has taught us, success comes from a combination of focus, determination, diligence, pure grit, a good dose of luck, and a touch of chutzpah. The successful entrepreneurs I've known possessed all of these qualities and one other characteristic that is seldom discussed—that of being an autocrat.

The reality of business today is that there are countless minefields along the climb to success. A seemingly innocent misstep in the wrong direction can spell not only disaster but also obliteration. Many a great idea has begun only to be stopped dead in its tracks by a miscalculation, lack of diligence, pure bad luck or timing—and typically a combination thereof. Many great companies that made it to the top began the start-up phase with a singular idea and one individual who knew that it was he or she who had to take the chance and pull the trigger. In nearly every case, deep down inside that person was a benevolent dictator.

On the surface, much of this may sound a bit nefarious. But in reality, navigating the path of a start-up venture is about as close as you can get to a 24/7 ride on the world's scariest roller coaster. Every morning, when the entrepreneur gets out of bed, it's show time. And every evening, when that same would-be tycoon restlessly drifts off to sleep, he or she says a silent prayer giving thanks for having survived the preceding 18 hours or so, and asking to be granted the strength to fight another day.

So what exactly *is* a benevolent dictator?

Well, the "benevolent" component means that the person always puts the entity, the employees, and, most important, the customer first—way ahead of him- or herself. Somebody has to take control in a start-up, and the trick is to ensure that this somebody can also be benevolent by doing the right thing for the right reasons, for all stakeholders.

The "dictator" piece of this designation simply means that— just as it is in a fast-tracked giant corporation—somebody in a new venture has to know when to say enough is enough. Debate, conversation, and analysis can take an organization only so far. The job of the entrepreneur, manager, or CEO is to say, "We're taking this fork in the road, for better or worse, and it's on my head." He or she is the one person who makes the important decisions when it counts—while others vacillate, the clock is ticking and resources are dwindling.

Most people cannot deal with this type of immense, almost constant pressure, and the monumental decisions that need to be made day in and day out. That's why so many companies often suffer from "analysis paralysis": the persistent indecision that usually leads to failure or plain old-fashioned inertia. It's a lot like treading water in the middle of a beautiful lake. You're doing fine until exhaustion sets in, and then you begin to sink like a rock. When you spend too much time trying to build consensus, you quite simply fail to accomplish anything that moves the venture forward, which will inevitably lead to a one-way trip to the bottom of a dark body of water.

My experience has been that although many individuals claim to want—and be able—to be a leader and make the big decisions, these claims usually fall short when push comes to shove. Indeed, most people just want to follow or be a bystander, because it's easier and much safer—and some simply want to get out of the way. I respect those people who know what they are and what they are not. It's the people who claim to be one thing and are another when put in a leadership position who cause the serious damage.

My management style is theatrical at times: It's intended to make the big point. It may even be hard-hearted and unrelenting when necessary for the greater good—but this is just another aspect of being a benevolent dictator. The real benefit of leading in this way is that it allows me to move faster than the competition and save time, money, and energy to capitalize on the opportunity. I know that I've made the decision, and the time for talking is done. One of the most important factors in business today is the ability to move from mind to market measured in hours and days instead of the usual weeks, months, and years.

I learned this trait growing up in Columbus, Ohio, when I was around 9 or 10 years old. I didn't go to camp in the summer like many other kids, because my family couldn't afford it. So instead, I played a lot of baseball in the streets. I learned early on that if I brought the ball and bat, the game started and ended when *I* decided. The same applies in business. Though I'm not a traditional consensus-builder type, that's not to say I don't try or that I'm not a team player. Building a consensus has its place—after the start-up process is a distant memory, when every dollar won't mean the difference between staying in the game and folding the tent. But when it's time for an "all-in" move, one person has to say "yes" to get things going.

Keep in mind that being a benevolent dictator doesn't mean being a jerk. You still need to sell people on your ideas and build champions who will follow you to the ends of the earth—not because they have to, but because they want to. Part of the trick is getting people to think that your idea is really their idea. However, that type of management style unfortunately doesn't work when you work for someone else and aren't making the final call.

Yet one of the best ways to hone your style is to work in a larger organization that you don't—and won't—own. It's a great way to gain the requisite experience on someone else's dime. Following this path has served me well while fueling my desire to lead rather than follow. With both OfficeMax and Max-Wellness—my most recent venture—being the benevolent dictator provided the critical leadership necessary to take an idea and transform it into reality as fast as possible, which is a huge competitive advantage.

Before co-founding OfficeMax, I spent about 15 years at Jo-Ann Fabrics now known as Jo-Ann Stores—the country's largest craft and fabric retailer. I started in a marketing position, and as I rose through the ranks during those 15 years, I moved up quickly to number two or three in the organization. Although I enjoyed my time there, I always felt that I could make a huge difference—and create a company that could better serve the customer—if I could do things my way. That is why, midway through 1985, I decided to take one shot to try to change the trajectory of Jo-Ann Stores and its leadership.

Over the years I had developed many good contacts and made many friends on Wall Street. One was the group at Drexel Burnham Lambert in Los Angeles, the then "go-go bankers du jour." I recruited a few Jo-Ann comrades to join me in California so that we could meet with a Drexel team and explore the possibility of taking Jo-Ann—at the time, a public company operating under the name Fabri-Centers of America— private through a leveraged buyout (LBO). After a series of discussions, Drexel gave me a nonbinding commitment, subject to full due diligence, for about $50 million to lead a buyout of the company.

That was all I needed to take the leap. We then went to the owners, explained the potential deal, and told them, "We can make you a lot of money."

The CEO thought it was a great idea and told me I could work with his son to take the company to the next level.

That wasn't exactly what I had been thinking. I wanted to run the show myself—make it a solo performance. Fortunately, I had gone into this proposed offer with a degree of confidence and from a position of strength. The first year that their son came into the company, I went to the owners—the Rosskamm family—and received a guaranteed payout contract. It provided that whenever I wanted to leave—or they wanted to fire me—I would receive several years' salary and benefits as though I had retired from the company. This gave me the cushion to make my move, knowing my family wouldn't starve to death (at least for a couple of years), no matter how my hand played out.

After my LBO offer fell on deaf ears and failed, I knew I'd have to do something different with my life. In reality, I suffered from a syndrome I call "too cushy too soon." By age 27 or 28, I was a senior vice president making a respectable six-figure annual income. As with any job, one gets good at it and can do it quickly after a while. As a result, I got bored my last couple of years at this fabric retailer, which had grown to more than 600 stores during my tenure. When I realized I'd never be CEO or own a big piece of the place, I started making plans to do something else. I needed to be my own boss. I also subscribed to the great singer Frank Sinatra's management style that teaches us to accomplish objectives using our own methods, as explained in the famous song "My Way."

In 1987 I started putting out feelers to Wall Street friends and business acquaintances that I was interested in an entrepreneurial challenge. I talked to people in New York and California, as well as Chicago and Cleveland. I decided that enough was enough and made a deal with the fabric company owners that called for me to leave the company on March 31, 1988. I gave the family almost six months' notice so that they could prepare for my departure. To this day, I like to say that OfficeMax was my April Fools' joke on the naysayers who said I couldn't do it—because

April 1, 1988, was the date on which we formally started OfficeMax.

It was in the fall of 1987 that I actually started making decisions about what I would do in my life after Jo-Ann. The most interesting opportunity that came my way was from the then-high-powered, certainly non-white-shoed street-fighter investment banking firm Bear Stearns. I had met Ace (Alan) Greenberg and a number of his managing partners over the years, which had led to discussions about my moving to New York City. Bear Stearns proposed to teach me investment banking and suggested that I could ultimately become a mergers and acquisitions banker focusing on the retail-chain sector based on my many years of experience.

Under normal circumstances, and if it had happened a few years earlier, that probably would have been the path I would have taken. But an important event had occurred a year earlier in 1986; I had married Ellen. She is very close to her family in Cleveland and, at that time, had her own professional career there. When I started talking about the attributes of the Big Apple and maybe moving to New York, Ellen was less than enthusiastic.

After leaving Jo-Ann, I maintained a close relationship with the entire Rosskamm family because of a lesson my late father, Lou Feuer, taught me—and that was to never burn a bridge. It's a lesson that I still not only preach, but also promote with my team. We can all have differences of opinion, but that does not mean we can't move on and still treasure past relationships. We should always value what we learned during our time in an association— which in my case provided building blocks for many of the ways I conduct business today.

I have also learned that in order to focus on building *anything*, you need a strong and supportive partner. For that reason, I knew that "peace in the family" must be a top priority—which caused me to look at other alternatives than moving to New York. The one that interested me most was figuring out how to become CEO of another retail chain in the Midwest.

I had offers to become president of several retail chains where, if I produced, I would be named CEO. But every company I spoke with left me stuck on the same issue—bureaucracy. There was no place for a benevolent dictator in the position of president of a traditional company; there was no feeling of entrepreneurship. And so, around the fall of 1987, I started thinking about starting my own retail chain. As luck would have it, a longtime acquaintance heard through the grapevine what I wanted to do and got in touch with me.

2

Lesson #2:
The Best Ideas Can Come
from What's Right in Front
of Your Nose

IN MY VIEW, some of the biggest—and occasionally easiest—money you can make in this world is often derived from the most obvious ideas. Think about two fairly significant music-playing devices: record players and the iPod. Each one is nothing more than a machine that plays the same kind of music that the likes of Frank Sinatra sang. The brilliance is in the distribution method, the ability to change it, and the capacity to capitalize on those changes by leveraging economies of scale and developing different packaging that makes owning the product "cool" to a new generation. When you really think about it, it's the same music; it's just a different way of sharing and listening to it. But both inventions required someone to look at the obvious and come up with the idea of creating a product—or better mousetrap—that people would both want and perceive they needed.

One fairly reliable reality in life is that most people will find reasons *not* to do something. They'll look for a way to keep the status quo and not challenge what can easily be tested or improved. It is the people who spend their time looking at what could be—based on the obvious—that rise above the rest.

However, even that kind of outlook doesn't always ensure success. Most people fail in the planning stage of a start-up venture because they make it much more difficult than it needs to be. Whatever you end up doing—whether it's selling something, developing a product, or finding a cure for cancer—it must first be something that people *want* and *need*. They may not know they want or need it yet; that's where marketing comes in. Creating a demand for a product is about communicating why it's a must-have item and what's in it for the customer.

Some of the best ideas—such as the ones in which I specialize—must be something so simple that they don't require a lot of time or effort to educate people about why they should want and need it. It's got to be something they see or hear about and say, "Yes, I get it, I want that." It might even evoke the feeling that "I can't live without it."

My ideal business would have been to enter the toilet paper industry. Why not? It's a product that most people use daily, and it's one that they keep buying and using until the day they die. In terms of a cradle-to-grave product, it doesn't get much better than this.

Ideas, in their most basic form, are like coffee or fine wine; you have to let them either percolate or age. You take something you think somebody may need and determine whether there's a market already in place for it. Or, you figure out if there is some way you can improve on how it's packaged and delivered, or whether you can create something from scratch to replace what's out there.

How do you do this? It's simple: You listen—specifically, to the people who are users and who'd be your customers. However, you also need to interpret what they mean, because people don't always say what they want, need, or are looking for in the exact words you'd hope to hear. My favorite way to conduct market research is to walk around and listen and talk to people in the obvious—as well as the strangest—places. My other approach is just to read—not necessarily what you'd read for your own enjoyment, but material that gives you clues to what might be of interest to people in the market you're considering serving. Talk on planes. Walk around. Go to other retailers. Watch TV. Read newspapers and magazines. Go on the Internet. Keep your eyes, ears, and mind open. It's really that simple.

My own method is a bit voyeuristic; I'm actually surprised I haven't been stopped by the police yet. I watch people's habits. I learn. I find out the answer to one basic set of questions: How do they do things, what are their needs, their concerns, and their sources of fear, satisfaction, and utter joy? After I've gathered these facts, I then begin to analyze how they do things and start thinking about how it might be done differently and more efficiently. I ask myself, what industry and new market could be created to improve upon what is already there?

This methodology applies to the process of creating most good ideas. You find a need—or where you think there's a need—learn what solution people currently have, and start inquiring as to whether there's a better way to do this than what's currently being done. Then you start to modify the idea and give it some time to germinate as you continue to ponder it from various perspectives.

I used to work out late in the evening—around 9 PM—in the early days of OfficeMax, jogging six—sometimes seven—days each week. I would use that roughly 45 minutes to ponder an idea. I'd start thinking about the problem and its possible solutions. It was a valuable exercise (pun intended) that produced incredible results.

I've found a fairly consistent habit when it comes to business ideas: Most people will talk themselves out of any solution before they reach it. They see the problem as a wall. They hit it and say, "Oh, somebody's most likely already thought of this." Then they give up and go back to the beginning and start with a different idea.

An entrepreneur is a completely different animal. If entrepreneurs have an idea they think is great, they see that wall and say, "Well, I can go over it, under it, or around it, or just knock the darn thing down. Okay, now how do I do that?"

That's the real difference between the people who make things happen and those who just talk about it. When you find that idea, you need to spend time thinking about how to nurture it and then figure out how to translate it into a reality. And damned be the walls that you face along the way.

In the beginning, you have a jumping-off point where you know the idea you've developed is viable and workable. You know that you want to take it from concept to something actionable. In order to make that happen you need resources, which come in many different forms—including time, money, and people. Resources are also your own and others' commitments to the idea.

The support you get from the people around you is critical. If you went to your husband, wife, or significant other and said, "I'm going to write the great American novel," your partner might say, "Terrific." But, if you added, "I'm going to quit my job and you're going to have to get a second job working at night flipping burgers to make ends meet," well, then their reaction might change a bit. You need your own dedication—and that of others in your life as well—in order to move an idea forward.

Some of the resources and initial commitment I was able to secure came from my meetings with another accomplished entrepreneur. I met with this operator, who was a wholesaler and distributor, during November and December 1987 as I was preparing for my exit from Jo-Ann Stores. My soon-to-be-partner had owned several companies over his career, and we initially discussed the viability of launching a retail chain. He had heard about Staples and Office Depot, two regional office supply start-up chains, and liked the idea of bringing this new concept to middle America. Although there were about 18 other companies in this space that had all launched within months of each other, none were big players yet. Where there wasn't an upstart superstore chain, those smaller, traditional office supply stores cared more about selling goods to the customers when they wanted to sell them—instead of focusing on when the customer wanted to buy them. They essentially lacked product depth and a variety of conveniences. Entrance into this industry made sense to my potential partner and me because the customer was being underserved and, in most cases, gouged by high prices.

Our idea was to create something different. We planned an office supply prototype that was bigger than life for the Midwest, where no other operators yet existed. Our stores would offer the products that home offices and small businesses wanted and needed, and we'd be open for them when they wanted to shop, without the usual restrictions. We would feature lower prices and better service than the other guys, and make it an exciting place to shop. We would bring the products to life by taking them out of the then-brown boxes, and put them on open display so people could touch, feel, and experience using them.

We knew that if we could do all that, we could replace those mom-and-pop office suppliers the same way supermarkets had replaced mom-and-pop grocery stores.

Ultimately, this way of thinking became a formula for an interloper like OfficeMax to spring up and fill an obvious void, initially in states like Ohio, Pennsylvania, and Michigan. Before we started, we went "to school" to learn from the things that Staples and Office Depot did right and wrong.

The deal between my partner and me was simple: I'd be the benevolent dictator, and he'd be the money-finder guy. And luckily for me, he was one of the best of the best. His job was to find the first-round investors to supply the funds necessary to get the business off the ground, and also to focus on the initial real estate selections. My job was to put all the pieces together to get the business moving, build the team, develop the marketing strategy, and work with banks and vendors. I would also serve as the closer for the investors because I had the 15 years of executive retail chain experience, which added requisite credibility to our undertaking.

We literally took a blank piece of paper and began working on what would eventually become OfficeMax. We believed that improving the state of office supplies was an obvious idea for a business; after all, it provided something people needed, wanted, and used every day.

However, after a relatively short time, we parted ways. It wasn't because I didn't like my partner or I wanted him to leave; it was simply a matter of style. He was what I then thought epitomized the gun-toting entrepreneur. He came on strong and got stronger. He was good at what he did, because the word "no" wasn't in his vocabulary. That applied to me, too, in some ways; however, I was also a strategist who used facts and figures, and then processed them with my head, my heart, and my gut to get to an answer. Though I admired his methods initially, I knew that in the long haul we were in—as they say—a marathon, and not a sprint. I could tell that his instant gratification style didn't mesh well with my more patient approach, which I felt would pay a much bigger dividend.

3

Lesson #3:
How to Find the Money to
Make Big Money

It TAKES MONEY to begin any venture. The necessary funds can come from a variety of sources—from the very mundane, such as digging into your own savings, or appealing to FF&A (friends, family, and affiliates). Another possibility is going to private equity types, including venture capitalists. I don't like the latter for a pure start-up because of the time and effort it takes to woo professional investors. They also tend to be much too skeptical for their own good, and often want to have too much influence. Although this certainly makes sense for them, it is not necessarily the best situation for the entrepreneur.

In addition to finding initial investors, ideally private individuals, who want to make 10-plus times their money, I have developed a few other unique twists to raise capital that have worked well for me, especially in the early stages of development.

These alternatives, although they are a bit unorthodox, have proven to be my most successful. They include attaining backing from suppliers, vendors, and landlords, and providing them with added incentives that serve both sides' needs. I have one simple rule when it comes to most things (that I mentioned in the Author's Note): "If you don't ask, you'll never get."

Raising money is an ongoing process when you're building a business—one that takes time and a lot of effort. Though most entrepreneurs don't like doing this, they must learn to live with the process, because it's a stark reality of growing a company. If a new business venture proves successful, more funds will be needed to take it to the next level. I resolved early on in my career that begging, borrowing, and creating a unique vehicle to raise money were just part of the game—and I learned to enjoy the process.

Individual circumstances dictate the direction one takes to obtain growth capital. If you don't have any money, the alternative becomes fairly straightforward: You get it from somebody else. The one thing I can guarantee is that no matter how much capital you have at the beginning, you'll always need more. Although this might seem illogical at first, it does make sense; the better the business and its initial success, the more times you'll have to go to the well for fresh capital to accelerate expansion, even though you might be making money. If you're hell-bent on growing, this is the way it works.

Some of the larger amounts of capital for a venture, after it starts to take root, come from another segment of what I call OPM—other people's money—which is covered in more detail in Chapter 35. And most savvy investors—particularly professional venture capitalists—want to make sure that the entrepreneur has "skin in the game." They want to know that if the venture fails, the entrepreneur will suffer—badly. That's all well and good. Most entrepreneurs need to combine their own funds with others', unless they are independently wealthy or have figured out how to select rich parents before birth.

One of the major myths I discovered when we were launching OfficeMax was that obtaining money was not, in fact, the most difficult obstacle; it was actually the easiest to overcome. It all comes down to a combination of the entrepreneur's concept, the plan's thoughtfulness, and sometimes—even to a greater extent—his or her passion and theatrical ability to present a cohesive story with a beginning, a middle, and a happy ending, all before the new company's first chapter has been written.

Every investor I ever met wanted to be a part of something that would succeed. Although this makes sense, of course, you can't dismiss the importance of the "hitch-their-wagon-to-a-star" factor. Money attracts money, and most investors want to go with the smart money, simply because it's smart business. The real trick is finding a stalking horse—in other words, getting a name-brand investor who has a track record of picking winners.

What may surprise novice entrepreneurs is that it is not all that terribly difficult to find this type of investor. This is quite simply because these types of investors have a sixth sense—a radar system, if you will—plus great networks of like-minded new idea hunters, and are always on the lookout for the next winner. Many times, the individual FF&A investor's association with a winning enterprise is just as important as the money that is being invested. I call this "bragging rights." These investors and their stories of successful ventures are much like fine wines; they get better with age and each time the story is repeated.

This Law of OPM worked well—no, make that *extremely* well—when we started raising capital for OfficeMax. The sheer reality at the time was that I had little money, and my partner had some. We realized that our combined resources would be a mere drop in the bucket of what we needed if we were going to make it big. We began to simultaneously refine the business plan and create our capital search strategy. We knew that the minimum amount of money we needed just to open the first three stores was about $3 million, plus a bank line and letter of credit.

The next step was to simply *do it*. We initially targeted friends, family, and affiliates. The original share price was $50, with a minimum investment of $250,000. Most new ventures that want to look like they're playing in the big leagues (or the "bigs") set a minimum; it makes it seem as though the entrepreneur is being highly selective, and that only "A" players need apply. The truth, however, is that practically every deal will drop this minimum if the prospective investors simply pause for more than 10 seconds.

Both my partner and I knew many successful people, and we decided to approach two key major constituencies: doctors and lawyers. Not only are these two professions typically comprised of bright people who created some degree of wealth, but they would give us stalking horses with credibility. This would facilitate our subsequent capital raises, which we knew would be required and would be just around the corner.

I had put in about $20,000; my co-founder invested around $100,000. Our investors received the preferred shares with all of the whistles and bells; we took common stock with no preferences. But the valuation and capital structure we established was such that the preferred owners' $3 million did not buy control of the company. Our shares controlled 51 percent of the business. We sold investors this structure because it ensured that they felt they won: The outside investors received many preferences in case of failure, because this group would get any assets remaining, before us, if we tanked. It was worth it, however, to us because we kept control.

On April 1, 1988, with cash in hand, we opened our offices in a building in a low-rent area of Wickliffe, Ohio—a blue-collar Cleveland suburb—and began what became a wild 15-year adventure.

4

Lesson #4:
Once an Entrepreneur,
Always an Entrepreneur

WHETHER IT IS true or not, there is a theory about entrepreneurs that seemingly plays itself out time and again: "Once an entrepreneur, always an entrepreneur." The business world is rife with serial entrepreneurs who have founded two, three, and sometimes four or more start-ups over their careers. Rarely does someone who is a true entrepreneur find satisfaction in hanging up his or her spurs when their initial start-up reaches the end of Phase Four with some sort of cash-out event.

Entrepreneurs have a knack—some would call it a need—for building and growing. This usually manifests itself in the form of companies. I have finally realized at some cerebral level that founding start-ups is something that must be hidden away somewhere in my DNA. In late 2008, five years after selling

OfficeMax, I couldn't sit still so I set out to launch my next great retail chain, Max-Wellness.

For the five years preceding Max-Wellness's launch, I had been a venture capitalist and retail consultant. These roles were primarily determined by the fact that I had a noncompete agreement that kept me out, for practical purposes, of the retail business—a business I much preferred over being a bystander-as-a-consultant type. I personally found it annoying just to offer advice and know that clients could take it or leave it. I was used to having it my way, and I hated biting my tongue for the sake of the big fees I received for simply giving my opinion rather than acting as the benevolent dictator who made things happen.

It was also during this time that I received far too many half-baked business ideas from way too many clueless people.

I also quickly joined a number of boards and started writing my monthly business column in *Smart Business* magazine and *Smart Business Online*, something I still enjoy doing very much. Though this added to my credibility, it also unfortunately attracted even more half-baked ideas to my doorstep. So as my five-year operating a retail chain noncompete contract with OfficeMax wound down, I started making plans to get back in the game.

As luck would have it, an accounting firm partner with whom I did some business called me out of the blue and asked if I would have lunch with one of his clients—who claimed to have the next great OfficeMax idea—and his client's attorney. I agreed to the lunch meeting, and met for the first time with a charming gentleman who would become my next business partner. He was a successful catalog operator who started as an entrepreneur and—unlike me—had never worked for anyone but himself.

The catalog operator, our accountant mutual friend, and the operator's attorney all showed up to present the big idea.

The catalog operator began explaining his vision of the future and the success he had achieved with his quasi health-care catalog. He said that the next big play in the United States would be wellness, and although the idea wasn't exactly earth-shattering, it was interesting.

I explained that I had to run the show in order to become involved. Further, I told them that even if I did, it wouldn't initially be with my own money. The lunch concluded with the catalog operator saying he was intrigued and would get back to me. The concept was a good one, and I fully recognized the mushrooming buying power of baby boomers, as well as the obsession the country was developing with wellness.

And there was another factor that piqued my interest. In 1988, when I was starting to think about office products, my other two ideas at the time were health care and the pet business. I always liked the health care play better, but didn't think that from a demographic perspective its time had come in 1988. Now things had come full circle. Better yet, it was time for me to get back into the game. After all, I was an entrepreneur, and that's what entrepreneurs do—build businesses.

5

Lesson #5:
It's Better to Be Lucky
Than Just Good

I'VE ALWAYS SAID that it is usually better to be lucky than good. However, there is a caveat in that statement: People who are lucky must be smart enough to be aware of their good fortunes so that they can take advantage of the opportunities before them. The timing with OfficeMax was exceptional, and we were lucky enough—read that as *smart enough*—to recognize the chance we had to be lucky. Once again this was proving to be the case with Max-Wellness.

After the lunch meeting, I was intrigued. Although many people seem to think that I have ice water in my veins and at times project a disinterested persona, I'm just a good negotiator who plays his cards close to the vest rather than getting all warm and fuzzy. Once someone knows where you stand, the price of poker usually goes up quickly. However, after the lunch I did what I always do when I don't know the answers. I took a deep dive into researching wellness and the future of health care. Most important, I needed to figure out where people would find Answers for Healthy Living (the Max-Wellness theme line) in the years ahead.

And so my interest grew.

The catalog operator called to schedule a meeting a few days after our lunch. When we met, I told him that I had done some homework, I did like the concept, and I might be interested. But I had some ground rules. I reminded him that I wanted to be the boss, call all the major shots, and not use my own cash to get this business started.

I had structured the deal so that he would put up the first $2 million for working capital, and I would own 25 percent as a starter, investing my time in lieu of hard cash. About six months later I renegotiated the deal. My partner gave me what was in effect another 25 percent in exchange for my need, because of the time required for the business, to give up my lucrative speaking engagements and consulting and devote the vast majority of my efforts to the new venture. My partner would eventually step out of the picture, but remain on the company's board of directors for a time until we opened the first four stores. After a couple of weeks and much wrangling, we finally crafted a financial structure that we both hoped would become the next mega-retail chain concept in the United States.

When we first envisioned Max-Wellness, now-President Barack Obama was a strong contender for the presidency—despite so many people's claims that he didn't have a chance. It is fair to say that after Obama was elected, his first and most vociferous priority became health-care reform. The reality is that there are approximately 50 million Americans who don't have health insurance. Depending on how one keeps score, this is somewhere in the vicinity of 15 to 20 percent of this country's population. Putting politics aside, most reasonable people in the United States agree that something must be done to care for this large segment of our population—and, equally important, to find a way to reduce everyone's health-care costs.

After selling OfficeMax, I got involved with University Hospitals of Cleveland, Ohio, the prime affiliate of Case Western Reserve University Medical School. Through the sponsorship of my longtime and close friend Dr. Fred Rothstein—physician and the President of University Hospital Case Medical Center—I received a seat on the board of directors. I decided during my first year that it was time for me to give something meaningful back to the community—and not just write a check. The hospital was enduring a large-scale and difficult, but very necessary, rebranding effort during this time, and a variety of circumstances led me to direct this undertaking on a de facto basis—working with doctors, administrators, and outside consultants.

I spent about 30 percent of my time getting really involved that year—probably, at times, to the chagrin of the hospital leadership (possibly Fred as well). I can't help it; I am what I am, and I don't do a job with any less than complete, 100 percent effort. As a result of this experience, I learned a lot about what worked in health care—and what didn't. Although I didn't know it at the time, this involvement also provided an excellent tutorial for the Max-Wellness start-up. In 2010 I also joined NCH Hospital System of Naples, Florida, where I have a home, as a member of its board of trustees.

As a marketer I always try to look at everything through the customer's eyes in an effort to find better ways of delivering goods and services. When you step back a few paces, it's usually obvious what it will take to get the job done—and make it a more satisfying experience for all involved.

As we began developing and then fine-tuning the Max-Wellness concept and go-to-market strategy in late 2008 and early 2009, it became clear that we were definitely in the right place at the right time. Virtually at no other time in history had health care and wellness received so much attention—be it in Washington, D.C., by the media, or by the person on the street, which is what appealed to me most. Fear can be a great motivator, and at some level the fear of not staying active and healthy tops the list of just about everybody once he or she reaches the age of 40.

It seemed that over a relatively short period of time, Americans decided that chronological achievement was not necessarily a point one had to reach—and then change their lifestyles. Sixty became the new 50; 50 became the new 40; and even younger people in their 30s decided that they were no longer bound by the rules of Mother Nature and the aging process. The vast majority of Americans determined that it was time for action—not just more empty talk about vitality. The past 10 years saw health food stores spring up in almost every community and city across the country. Exercise became an important part of the active lifestyle, and people began to enthusiastically address topics such as healthy eating, preventing obesity, smoking cessation, and countering other contributors to poor health and reduced life spans.

Laws changed. Food-labeling requirements tightened both for packaged goods in the grocery store and, in most states, for restaurants. A new wave of smoking prohibitions in public places also began to take hold. Who would have thought that bistros, bars, and restaurants in cities like New York City and Los Angeles would no longer be havens for those who practiced the social ritual of ingesting noxious gases into their lungs?

Max-Wellness was certainly lucky that the topic of health—the entire focus of our new business—gained top-of-mind awareness from coast to coast and around the world. We watched with admiration as politicians debated how to provide health care, and consumers began to explore how to utilize the various tools available to them in attempts to discover what Ponce de Leon tried to find in the sixteenth century: the Fountain of Youth.

6

Lesson #6:
"GOYA"—The Only Way to
Really Test an Idea

SO YOU HAVE this idea that you think will work. You even have a champion or two who will help you bring it to life. Then what? Well, don't hire research people just yet to borrow your watch to tell you what time it is—in other words, the obvious. You should instead begin by undertaking a process in which I'm a big believer: GOYA, or Get Off Your Ass.

GOYA means that you take that idea and start testing it. You go to places where people shop and buy; walk around and watch how they do it. You envision how your idea would make it better, easier, and faster for people to do something that they're currently doing poorly, with difficulty, or slowly. You see if your concept has legs. Most important, you determine how to make your idea work, and how to improve it. It is imperative that you don't fall in love with the "how"—just with the expected results. Though every great idea starts in a particular way, most take an unexpected turn—usually several—along the journey. Those entrepreneurs who fail are the ones who neglect to keep an open mind and don't constantly conduct their own smell tests to ensure that things are falling into place.

We opened our first OfficeMax store in the Cleveland suburb of Mayfield Heights, Ohio. The main reason that we chose this location was because it was close to both the office and my home. I knew I had to be close to the location, because I wanted to visit as often as possible. After all, a first store is much more than brick and mortar; it's a laboratory with an ongoing search for discovery.

When the store first opened I would go there seven days a week and just hang out. I would shake hands with all of the working associates to be polite, and then I would go about my mission. I was there for one key purpose: to learn. I'd go to the office Monday through Saturday, then go home, change out of my suit and tie and into a pair of jeans or khakis. Around 7:30 PM, I'd then head to the store and do my best Inspector Clouseau routine, just walking around, trying to understand how people shopped. I learned about such things as the clocks on the walls, the bags people carried out of the stores, and the shopping carts they pushed up and down the aisles. Sunday differed only because I was already in casual garb.

Most people think great ideas come with a bolt of lightning. Let me tell you something: There's no lightning. Great ideas are born of a simple combination: understanding how to find good ideas, and being aware of what you're seeing. You also have to be an adept interpreter, because most people's words don't tell you what they really mean. You must instead translate what they're saying into what they're trying to communicate by watching the body language they provide when they talk, such as the tone of their voice, their gestures, and their facial expressions.

You have to begin to fine-tune your idea and see if the modifications work. The only way to do this properly is to test it first—before you pour tons of money into it, launch a business, and then find out that it's doomed to fail or that the competition is already light-years ahead of you. Testing it is a core principle of building a business; you and your team have to see what's going on with your own eyes, internalize it, and analyze it. And you have to figure out what exactly it all means. Only then do you reach the point where you can begin to perfect your initial idea.

Once you complete the preliminary work, you must begin to formalize the idea by asking what it will look like. I don't believe in spending all my time and effort on a formal business plan, because I have never seen one exactly hit the bull's-eye. You're either under, over, or way off the target. My theory is that a plan is a metamorphosis. You get an idea in the start-up phase. Then you start to imagine the "what if?" scenarios while you ask yourself how you might put things together. It's as simple—and difficult— as that. But you *absolutely* have to get off your rear end in order to do it.

We continued to tweak our plan for Max-Wellness in an attempt to determine how best to position the company as the top, preferred provider of goods and services that would become synonymous with health and well-being. We planned to take advantage of the country's obsession du jour, which seemed to promise decades of sustained appeal.

As an entrepreneur, I try not to fixate on the problem or the "spin." Instead, I try to look at things from the perspective of a pilot, race car driver, or motorcycle rider: I know anyone who fixates will inevitably succumb to what is a proven concept of target fixation. "Target fixation" is a known psychological malady that was first discovered during World War II in pilots who would stare at—or fixate on—a target. Lo and behold, they would—unsurprisingly—crash into that target. The same goes for race car drivers who look at a guard rail and then hit it, as well as motorcycle riders who stare right below the front wheel. All will quickly find themselves looking up from the pavement (provided they are still conscious).

I therefore take a different approach to avoid the consequences of this predicament: I attempt to determine what the problem or opportunity is, and then instead of focusing on it, I simply look far enough down the field or the road to develop possible solutions. I am always thinking of pitfalls and benefits when I am imagining solutions, because these go hand in hand when breaking new ground. Once I think I might have something that works, I use my technique for floating trial balloons. To test the waters, I put forth statements in various contexts: media interviews and speeches, public gatherings, and one-on-one meetings with people within the company, external vendors, suppliers, and consultants. Friends and family are also never spared.

As an opportunist, my objective was to determine how to hitch Max-Wellness's wagon to the star—in this case, the country's new focus on staying well to live well.

Once I reached the point where I was ready to really commit, one of the important next steps was to hone a position statement that included the who, what, why, where, and how Max-Wellness would fit the customers' needs.

I structured the Max-Wellness concept as "the solution provider," regardless of what legislation was passed. The truth is that anyone in their right mind wants to be well. By positioning Max-Wellness as the provider of Answers for Healthy Living, we were making a bold statement.

I was asked by reporters in a number of trade paper interviews what I—a newly self-crowned wellness expert—thought were the most important steps people could take for their own health. I'm sure, given that we were in the midst of the 2009 H1N1 veil of fear, many reporters thought that I would promulgate that people should do this, do that, take this, take that, and do whatever it required to fend off swine flu.

But that wasn't how I answered their questions. Whenever I deal with the media, I am constantly searching for the phrase, sound bite, or statement that will differentiate my company from others. So after reading a great deal about physicians talking about how to live healthier lives and what to do or not do—and listening to commentators talk ad nauseam about washing one's hands—I decided there was a much more salient point that would ring true with the United States.

So when I was asked to give my tip of the day on health care, I stated that my number one piece of advice on health care would be to "take responsibility for our own well-being and the well-being of our loved ones." I would amplify that statement by emphasizing that "each of us must first depend on ourselves, certainly not the government or our employees. Instead, we all must take responsibility to lower the cost of treatment by working harder and smarter to stay healthy, and thus avoid the need for treatment in the first place."

This seemed to resonate with the interviewers as soon as I uttered the words.

I've learned over the years that speaking the obvious and creating an action-oriented phrase doesn't just help to gain traction with the message's recipients. It also works wonders with important editors who have an insatiable appetite for catchy headlines.

In addition, my experience as an entrepreneur has allowed me to recognize that the media are in the business of providing information. As such, they need a constant flow of material to fill the airwaves, their pages, and, nowadays, their web sites. This is an important lesson for entrepreneurs, as it doesn't do one much good to have great ideas or a terrific product unless others know about it. Though I noted this earlier in the Author's Note, it bears repeating: You can't flirt in the dark.

The bottom line at Max-Wellness during the idea-planning stages was that we had an idea that no one else had yet introduced, and we had basically reached the point where we knew that the idea was sound. We just had to package it, which meant determining what the constituents would perceive about the entity we were creating.

After you've established your business concept, determining what goes into the package becomes much more important. The wrapping becomes superfluous once the bow is removed. But, in the beginning, a pretty bow does wonders.

Buoyed by our timing and our commitment to success, we knew we had something. Now it was a matter of executing a strategy that we could tweak along the way. We were dealing with people's lives, so one of my biggest concerns was the concept of "First, do no harm." It is what all doctors pledge to do when they take the Hippocratic oath and promise to practice medicine ethically throughout their careers. We went to great lengths to be sure that every product that we considered was efficacious, meaning that it actually *did* something. And even if it wasn't 100 percent successful, we wanted to make sure that it would certainly not hurt anyone. We also formed a medical advisory committee to point us in the right direction.

7

Lesson #7:
Don't Underestimate the Power of Focus, Discipline, and Follow-Up

ANOTHER OF MY favorite phrases: In the land of the blind, the one-eyed man or woman is king or queen. This certainly applies to business. People ask, "How did you ever make it so big?" (Which can be loosely translated as, "You're no brighter than I am, so how did you become so rich, and do it so quickly?")

The answer is focus. It's what you do with your head and how you think about what you have to do and how to do it. And once you figure it out, you improve on it again and again. Do you work to live or live to work? The right answer is both, depending on the time and place you're at in your life, as well as the building process. The goal is to have it "both ways, your way."

The start-up was my painter's canvas; and I knew that I was limited only by my imagination, energy, and inclinations.

In order to move your idea from start-up to the next phase of building it out, the idea has to have a real chance of becoming reality. That requires a combination of focus and follow-up. I might have been a good Marine except that I don't like authority. Discipline and process are the secret to getting to the next steps.

For example: Notes are mandatory for every meeting that I have. I'll frequently dictate the notes from a meeting the second I walk out (except for the cases in which someone else has been appointed scribe). I also keep a binder (nowadays, more electronic than paper) in which to keep these notes. And I always make sure that my notes include next steps. I designate the initials "FU" and a date under each section. When new people joining my companies get a copy of this, they sometimes think I'm giving them an ultimatum until they quickly realize that FU is not a pejorative, but instead stands for *follow up* by a certain date.

The following are my requirements for those who receive my notes or attend my meetings: I tell them, "I am not your father. When you tell me you're going to do something, you have to do it. However, you always can come back to me and say one of three things: 'I can't do it on time.' 'I don't want to do it your way, and this is why.' Or you can tell me you think it's a stupid idea and we shouldn't do it at all."

My number-one rule is: "Don't ignore me." It is a lesson my people are taught only once, and I've never had an associate forget it once they understood my objective and the consequences. I also give homework assignments and keep a running tally of what happened or changed from previous sessions on the same topic or project.

When you take the time to focus, have discipline, and require follow-up, you're creating a road map that documents what has to be accomplished and by when. Few things ever fall through the cracks when you follow this process.

I've come to learn from this approach that most five-year plans don't work; the world is simply evolving too fast. Instead, companies must have a short-term plan—that's survival; an intermediate plan—that's the one that tells you how to "get through the year"; and a long-term plan—that's the goals, benchmarks, and posts that you need to reach along the way. Think in terms of 3 to 6 months for short term, 7 to 18 months intermediate, and then long term as a couple of additional years. You should know, however, that you'll almost certainly have to modify the longer-term strategy.

I've found that most companies and their executives spend way too much time thinking about what's going to happen 5 or 10 years down the road. The ability to abandon a plan when necessary, change quickly, and deal with the unexpected is what makes a good business great.

A key tenet to keep in mind is that you cannot rely on a shotgun approach—trying to cover a wide area, hoping something resonates with your broadly defined target audience. I prefer using a rifle with a telescope to home in on a narrower target. Not doing so can be particularly precarious for a start-up, because every company or organization at one time begins with the proverbial blank piece of paper. The leaders of a start-up team must use that stark white sheet to delineate what they're going to do, how they're going to accomplish it, how they will measure success, and who will do what. All of this requires extreme and unrelenting focus.

Though there are some advantages to a shotgun approach, they rarely apply to ventures built from scratch. When you use a shotgun, you'll usually hit something. But the price in doing so seldom provides an adequate payback, which makes shotguns more useful when your resources are plentiful. I maintain that a laser-sharp attack is much more practical, productive, and economical. Using a laser takes much more planning, and it probably isn't as much fun as just picking up the shotgun and screaming, "Ready, fire, aim," instead of the traditional sequence. However, when a company transposes the aim and fire components it typically wastes a great deal of time and incurs extraneous costs. At that point, you'll have lost your focus, along with your discipline.

8

Lesson #8:
Competition Stinks

BEFORE WE OPENED our first OfficeMax store, we faced an initial challenge of figuring out how to enter the marketplace when there were 18 other newly minted superstore chains in the business. Personally, I think competition stinks, although it's not politically appropriate to say this. So does the concept of picking on someone your own size. That implies a 50/50 chance of success, and that isn't good enough for me. Therefore, I spent a lot of my time thinking about how to move the odds in my favor.

To change the odds, one has to change the positioning of the company, the brand, and the offering to differentiate it from the others. This gives the customer a real choice instead of simply a "me, too" alternative.

We at OfficeMax decided to focus on the Rust Belt—an area covering parts of the northeastern United States, mid-Atlantic states, and portions of the eastern Midwest—and gain strength there before playing in anybody else's backyard. Our goal was to have no competition the first two years. We came up with the idea to have three stores in Cleveland, Ohio, and then open locations in Buffalo, New York, and Detroit, Michigan.

Every company, every institution—every anything—always believes somewhere deep down inside that the competitor is smarter, better, or stronger. I don't care if it is Microsoft, Walmart, Intel, or Mercedes-Benz; I guarantee that they are all borderline paranoid, thinking that even the most minuscule competitor is gaining on them. In many respects, a small to moderate dose of paranoia is a good thing, because it forces organizations to change, improve, grow, innovate, and execute.

Although it's helpful to watch your competitor's every move—and fear of failure isn't bad—too many organizations spend too much time looking over their shoulders. They waste an inordinate amount of energy on repeatedly asking, "What if?" Instead of devoting time and effort in this woulda, coulda, shoulda exercise in futility, select your priorities and decide how you want to be positioned before your competitors do it for you. The way to beat the competition is to pick your battles and fight them at the time and place that *you*—not they—choose.

As I stated earlier, I am not big on "fair fights." I believe that it's preferable to find your strength by taking advantage of the other guy's weakness. This is especially true in the first phase of any business. Eschewing this is a sure way to kill a company and potentially ruin an idea before it ever gets out of the starting blocks.

A smarter approach is to figure out how a David can take on a Goliath and prevail. First, identify your competitors and learn everything there is to know about them. Read every word ever published; study their press releases and their ads. Talk to their customers, employees, supporters, and detractors.

When you are done, do it again, but this time read and listen between the lines. Think about how your organization is different, along with what works and what doesn't. The competition has many of the same issues you have. The difference is that, by doing your due diligence, you can crack the code for an effective work-around and turn a negative into a positive.

And don't believe every word that is written. A company's public relations and projected persona can be mighty weapons in diverting attention so that competitors don't focus on what is really happening behind the curtain. When you are done, you will more than likely discover one or more of their Achilles' heels.

Pick your spot. If the competitor claims to be able to custom-make its widget for a customer in 30 days, your position could be to promote that your product is ready for immediate delivery, because it is custom-designed for Industry X.

You must package the message in a way that hits the target's needs. If your larger nemesis promotes its 24/7 computerized answering service with artificial intelligence, announce that your company assigns a real, live, personal service rep to every client. Every situation almost always has more than one key positioning possibility.

Once you have the answer, aim your positioning statement where you will get the biggest bang for your buck. Small marketing budgets can go a long way toward producing big results when a laser-like approach is employed. If, for example, you are trying to reach left-handed, freckle-faced accountants, don't spend big money buying a spot during the Super Bowl to reach tens of millions of people, most of whom don't have an interest in what you are pitching. Instead, run your ad in the *Left-Handed, Freckle-Faced Accountants' Almanac*. Finally, be sure that everybody on your team is tuned in and turned on. Some of the biggest positioning failures occur because management didn't send the message to the troops before launching the big idea.

In order to succeed, an organization must deliver on the promise it makes. Every person in the organization needs to not only hear the message from the top, but also understand it, buy into it, and then live by it.

Plan your launch, pay attention to every detail, and listen for the fat lady of success to sing. Savor the notion that the board of directors in Goliath's ivory tower is no doubt telling its people that you are smarter, stronger, and better than they will ever be.

Remember, many a battle can be won with a well-aimed slingshot.

Phase Two

Build Out and Put the Idea to the Test

9

Lesson #9:
Business Is a Series of "Go" and "No-Go" Decisions

ANOTHER OF MY favorite singers, Kenny Rogers, unknowingly provided some of the best business advice I've ever learned. He sang—in reference to a hand of poker—"You got to know when to hold 'em; know when to fold 'em; know when to walk away; and know when to run."

The simple truth is that too many business owners start with what they believe is a great plan for success and charge full speed ahead. They're focused solely on the finish line, and don't appreciate the sheer number of obstacles that stand between them and their goals.

In theory, running flat out toward the finish line is great. But few things in business—or in life—go exactly as planned. The secret to survival is keeping an eye out for the mile markers along the way and learning how to recognize the signs that tell you something has to give, change, or even, occasionally, stop.

You'll inevitably encounter some delays on the path to building a successful company. There is real wisdom in being able to tell when it's time to reevaluate the game you're playing. This may constitute a full stop—folding your cards and cashing in the remainder of your chips. Or, it might mean taking just one part of the plan and reconstructing new replacement pieces.

As Rogers so eloquently described in "The Gambler," the cards don't always fall into place in the way you want them to. Part of the trick of successful entrepreneurship is remembering that a start-up—much like a card game—is comprised of a series of hands. Learning how to play the hands you're dealt rather than just judging the individual cards will allow you to come out a winner, especially when you start folding bad hands and strategically tinkering with the average and good ones.

Smart entrepreneurs run businesses with their head, heart, and gut. On a great day, all three kick in and you're rolling. Even on a bad day, you can continue to make progress as long as one of these faculties is still functioning. It is only when all three simultaneously stop and you're not sure why that you'd better recognize it's time to fold the hand. You need to be smart enough to stop, think, and listen—much like dealing with writer's block.

"Go" and "no-go" decisions, deadlines, and timelines all possess a common inherent danger: You try to meet them with no quality control in place because you feel obligated to get them done exactly as you had originally planned. Smart poker players don't force a losing hand and hope that it turns into a winner. Sure, they can bluff, but not too often. Similarly, you can normally get *something* done when you're low on chips, but the danger is that you start playing scared and the quality of what was originally intended could suffer.

You must modify your timelines as the game moves along, sometimes picking up the pace in one area while slowing down or stopping in another. A benevolent dictator's role in a start-up company is to be that traffic cop who knows when to say enough is enough. Often in an entrepreneurial venture, you will reach that inflection point when you just know in your heart and gut that you're ready to take that critical step from start-up to implementation, or are at least ready to start *thinking* about how to do so. You've determined that your idea is sound, and believe that you can translate it into a functioning business and bring your concept to market. You have a little bit of capital at your disposal, at least enough to take you to the next waypoint. This moment is a lot like falling in love: When it happens, you feel it, smell it, and know it.

Welcome to Phase Two of the adventure; this is when you have to make the critical go or no-go decisions.

At this juncture, you are faced with the decision of whether to pull the pin or take the next major step. You're probably scratching your head and asking yourself, "Does my concept still make sense?" If it doesn't, is it time to rethink your strategy and head in a different direction? Or should you just throw in the towel, suck it up, and go home?

In my experience, you abandon your cause when you discover through your evolution that you are sitting on a bad idea. You might realize that you can't fund it or find the right people. Maybe you don't have the stomach to see the idea through to the culmination when you flip the switch or open the doors and the cash register will start ringing.

Many budding entrepreneurs lose even more money and waste excessive time and energy beyond their initial investment because they don't have the guts to say, "I can't go any further." I've been involved in numerous deals where I walked away and then came back one or two years later to make it happen under even better terms and conditions than originally envisioned. This is not unique in business; in fact, it's nothing more than timing. I have also learned that some of the best deals are the ones you walk away from. If you have to work a deal too hard and things are not coming together, you'll intuitively feel that it is just not meant to be.

One example of this is when I was running OfficeMax and we were trying to acquire BizMart, a retail office supply chain that was bigger than we were. Just after we made a deal with the venture capitalist group that owned BizMart for about $300 million, another buyer surfaced and outbid us. I received a call late on a Friday night from my investment banker explaining what had happened and asking if we wanted to counter.

It took me about two minutes to decide to pass. As much as I wanted the deal—it would have doubled the size of OfficeMax— in my heart of hearts, I knew that the economics no longer worked and that if we proceeded, we would have to work our way out of a deep hole.

The entity that made the higher bid was named Intelligent Electronics. They were headquartered in the Philadelphia area, and had decided to jump onto what they thought was a retail gravy train. The following morning I called Intelligent's CEO and told him that I thought he had made a huge mistake. I asked him to write down my phone numbers and to call me when he realized what I already knew—that it would take a year for him to recognize that this acquisition would become his worst nightmare.

The CEO uttered a string of words that don't belong in a book of this quality, and then slammed the phone down in my ear. I knew then and there that this guy couldn't take a joke.

A year passed. Then, sure enough, I received a call one day from Intelligent Electronics (whose name defied the way it operated, as the company has long since gone out of business). The CEO sheepishly admitted that I had been right, and told me that he was ready to sell us BizMart. Rather than gloat, I listened closely as he explained how his company didn't really understand retailing and had lost a significant amount of money trying to make BizMart work. Worse, he had degraded BizMart's value and brand through a series of missteps.

I told him I was interested in taking the chain off his hands.

At the time, Kmart owned the majority stake in OfficeMax, which provided us with capital for acquisitions. I began negotiating with the CEO and arranged to send one of my vice presidents to BizMart's headquarters in Dallas and start the preliminary due diligence process. I gave the VP marching orders that he should find an out-of-the-way place and blend in upon his arrival.

My executive arrived to find chaos running rampant throughout the chain. Of course, that changed the dynamics of the offer I was considering and gave me a huge opening to dramatically reduce the size of our potential offer.

After doing the two-step with the CEO for a while, negotiations broke off. Intelligent Electronics' headquarters was far removed from BizMart's Dallas offices and its retail division, so BizMart executives didn't get word that talks had stalled. I had instructed my VP to stay under the radar, so no one seemed to notice he was still there and didn't ask him to leave. He kept doing his due diligence from ground level, reporting in every day and asking whether he should return to Cleveland. I said, "No way! Don't leave until management throws you out."

By the time we started negotiations again, we had uncovered even more information about the company. As a result, I was ready to drop the offer for BizMart by about $25 million. The CEO had no idea. I invited him to Cleveland to try to close the deal. The

CEO and his team flew to Cleveland and met me at OfficeMax's law firm of Baker & Hostetler in downtown Cleveland.

Robert Markey—one of Baker's best and brightest partners and my longtime friend, who has since passed away—was there with a bunch of our investment bankers. We were waiting in an office overlooking the airport and I was planning to drop my little bomb in the form of our lower offer—reducing it from the $300-plus million to about $275 million.

When the CEO and his entourage arrived, we all sat down and exchanged pleasantries. I waited about three minutes, and then suggested that the CEO and I speak privately in other room before we tried to close the deal. I had learned from Kenny Rogers that you could read the cards "by the way one holds his hands," and in the early stages of my talks with this particular chief executive, I had noticed that he had a set of telling habits that provided signs about what he was really thinking. For example, when he was bluffing, stretching the truth, or didn't have a clue about something, he would start to slide down in his chair; and the bigger his bluff, the deeper his slide. In addition, when he was talking and making something up on the fly, his Adam's apple began to gyrate up and down.

So here we were, just the two of us, and I'm watching his body slide up and down in a chair while his Adam's apple bobbed around like crazy. After he finished talking, I told him I was dropping the price of our offer by about $25 million. He nearly went ballistic. He then stood up, walked into the next room where everyone was waiting, and motioned to his people that they were leaving. Together, they walked to the elevator in silence.

My team and I watched from the window as the group climbed into a white stretch limousine and headed back to the airport, and even remained in the boardroom to see the plane take off from the nearby airport. I pondered in the back of my mind whether the CEO was mad enough to somehow strafe the building before his jet disappeared over the horizon.

Despite its unpleasant nature, there's a lesson to be learned from this minidrama. When you sit down at the table, you have to be able to change your bargaining strategy when the opportunity arises. You have to know when a deal is just too much work or just too painful to accept. You also have to determine your top price in advance, and when to push the chair from the table, get up, and walk away—or sometimes even run—if the deal just isn't falling into place. You must come from a position of strength rather than one of need. In this instance, my strength came from the information I gathered. My VP in Dallas was continually feeding me facts and figures that bolstered our position—information that, even to this day, I don't think the CEO ever knew we had.

That leads to another belief that I mentioned earlier. I'm a big proponent of theatrics, especially in negotiations. Done correctly, they can keep the other side guessing. I tell people all the time that one of my favorite business books is *The Red Badge of Courage*. The main character in this book is a coward—a 17-year-old soldier in the midst of the Civil War. Away from his camp he encounters a soldier from the same side who accidentally hits him in the head with a rife butt. He returns to his own camp covered in blood and the other, equally young soldiers assume that he's been in a battle—and he quickly becomes a hero in their eyes because he had been in combat. By the end of the story, the soldier does become a real hero, even though he spends much of the story acting the part until it becomes reality.

To be successful in business, you have to understand how to set the stage and play out your scene in order to make your impression on the other side. Sometimes you're engaged in the good guy–bad guy act. During others, you need to do something so outrageous that the other side cannot accurately even begin to predict your next move. The key is to never be backed into a corner, and never become predictable. Make sure that you're in control of the proceedings, and always be prepared to walk away when you recognize that things aren't working to your advantage. Usually, walking away will facilitate setting the tone and will get the opponent to march to your drumbeat rather than his. But, as I've emphasized throughout this book, in some cases, the best deal is the one you never make.

10

Lesson #10:
Treat an Idea Like Clay

THE PROCESS OF pursuing an idea is a lot like putting a complicated puzzle together one piece at a time. There is not necessarily a linear progression to assembling it. Larger, more complicated puzzles may require a team that can work together, with each member trying to fit the various pieces into the right places until a clear picture emerges.

One benefit to using a team approach is that you can assign tasks, which is similar to movie-making in some respects. Producers and directors film the scenes out of sequence, depending on economics or availability of actors, and then put it all together in the right order in the cutting room.

The same can be applied to creating a business. You determine the most efficient and effective path available, and then take it based on the availability of resources, including people and money. I have found that definitive business plans that do not include flexibility generally don't work well. There are always many moving pieces, and changes must be made quickly—sometimes on the fly, and as often as weekly and sometimes daily—to avoid dead ends before you complete a project. Entrepreneurs often fail here because they fall in love with their plans, not the intended results or the benefits to their customers or investors. They refuse to deviate or adapt, to reshape the idea and rework the plan.

To this day I have yet to see a plan that produces precisely what the entrepreneur originally thought or financial results that were originally projected. When we launched OfficeMax, we planned to open a total of 100 stores. We missed those projections by a factor of 10 and ended up with more than 1,000 stores in less than 10 years. Moreover, we were able to beat those projections because we seized the opportunities that were presented to us, and we reshaped the idea as we went along.

The best way to move faster—from mind to market, where you can build something of value—is to flex your idea and constantly search for ways to not only improve but also find add-on opportunities that will fit with the initial concept. That may sound contradictory—letting something stay fluid when you're trying to move fast—but think of an idea as clay. Like clay, you must constantly shape and reshape it over and over before you put it in the kiln to bake. As you keep pushing and pulling the idea along, molding it and improving it, you get much smarter. And the smarter you get through experience and new information, the faster you can move. You will pull the idea in different directions just to see what it looks like. When you don't like something, you can tweak it—and then you can tweak it again. I spend half my life playing "What if?" self-mind games, pondering alternatives and better ways that can all lead to a breakthrough discovery.

I continued to reinforce this message to our Max-Wellness team. I told them that we'd be agog at how little we knew one year from the first store opening—how what we thought was absolutely vital simply didn't work, and what we thought would never fly took off and soared. For example, I met with our product people and said, "Our business at Max-Wellness is three things: enhancing qualities of life, enhancing prevention, and providing treatments."

I then asked them to restate in their own words what they thought these three pillars of our concept meant. They were thinking literally about what I said, interpreting them as vitamins, staying fit, and the like. I had to stop them and say, "No. It's even simpler than that. Instead, think about wellness like this."

One of the best ways to stay well, I explained, is that first you shouldn't let yourself get in a bad situation—such as failing to eat right, exercise, or get enough rest. I told them that we were going to merchandise the store based on solutions, not products. I wanted them to think about wellness in terms of a completely different context—to stretch and reshape its meaning.

The team's marching orders were to think about what products—aside from the obvious ones—could connect the dots for our customers. The results included new soft services for seniors, such as using a third-party company we could retain on behalf of senior-age customers to safety-proof their homes so that they could continue living independently. Although this is certainly not what one might initially include in a store, we asked ourselves: Why not? The seniors or their caregivers visiting the store needed this service, and by establishing ourselves as a solution provider, this was a logical service extension for Max-Wellness. At its core, this idea—and all of the ideas for the company—became a combination of enhancing life, wellness, prevention, and treatments.

Reshaping ideas is an all-too-frequently underestimated process in business. However, it's a relatively simple concept. You draw a box around an idea and then seed other ideas in and outside the lines. They are not all going to work; you won't pursue every single one of them. After all, if you do 10 things that all work perfectly, you're not doing your job—because you're only doing the obvious, easy ones and not taking enough chances. Not every chance you take is going to prove workable—and that's okay. Merely putting your team in "exploration mode" provides the opportunity for that single discovery that can provide a huge payback.

To really create new ideas and forge new ground, you must take certain actions that could potentially fail. However, when you fail early, you can fix things and move on. Failures in and of themselves will not put you out of business if you manage the risk. Any good operator will have tried a few things that didn't produce as expected—and some will even fall flat. Part of treating ideas like clay is that you actually want to involve products and services among your offerings that allow you to troll for the next great idea—the one that suddenly, for some almost magical reason, gels with your customers.

There are a number of ways to mitigate the economic downside of shaping and reshaping ideas, including working with your vendors and suppliers. I like to call this method *merchandise on a string* in retailing; however, we usually refer to it as *collaborating* when we speak to vendors, because this makes it sound more palatable to them.

One example from the early days of OfficeMax is how we sold cellular phones. At that time, people thought of a cellular phone as nothing more than a phone that was mobile and didn't have a cord connected to the wall. It was well before the days of the multitasking smartphones of today. So we figured we could stretch the idea of a phone without a cord to include additional products that made using the phone better, such as hands-free speakers (which are now commonplace) and earpieces that allowed drivers to keep both hands on the wheel.

The other part of the equation is learning when it's worth taking a calculated risk, but also how to mitigate it. One way to do that is to find a partner.

You can go to a vendor and say, "Mr. Vendor, I want to do this speaker kit idea with cellular phones and different types of cords and other stuff because I think there is a need even though it's never been done before." And then you lay out the deal: "If it fails, we share the risk. We're going to give your products the valuable shelf space and train our associates on how to sell your stuff. However, we're not going to pay for the products during this test period until they sell. When the idea works, you will have a new avenue for your products; you can even pitch the product to others besides us. We win as well because we've taken a linear step forward. If the idea fails, we will keep trying until we find a winner."

I've seldom had vendors say no when I've approached partnerships this way. In fact, the smart vendors jumped at the opportunity for us to, in effect, do their customer research.

Another example of reshaping ideas occurred during the 1980s, when everything was in a box in U.S. office supply stores. A customer would walk into a store and find the products packed in plain containers. The front of the box revealed the contents, such as the word *ink*. If that was what one was looking for, that was what was purchased—without ever opening or examining the product.

I saw this and thought to myself: "What about the other thousands of items that were sold that people didn't even know existed?"

So we decided to add a sense of drama and theater to the store and the products. Just like a 1920s Sears catalog, we provided information about the features and benefits of the merchandise live and in person. We took the products out of the box and put them on the shelf. And then we invited customers to touch, play with, and test out the products, emphasizing our thought that "Seeing is believing."

Over the years, we developed many ways to market products at OfficeMax that involved allowing people to learn how to use them right there on the store shelves. We took this approach with fax machines, phones, printers, even writing instruments. Reshaping the context of the products we were selling allowed us to become the first Midwestern retailer to have pens with a string attached to them so that you could test every pen we sold. That is the kind of walk-around, look at your shoes, low-hanging fruit, easy-things-first method of restructuring basic concepts.

From there, the idea becomes an accordion and expands. All of a sudden, you've taken a seemingly boring idea of selling pens in a plain box—without allowing customers to tell what the pen felt like to hold—and transformed it into an experience where customers could take the product for a "test write."

Idea shaping, and reshaping, is simply a matter of tweaking and fine-tuning. I have never worked on any business or personal project—or anything of value—in which I have been 100 percent satisfied at the end of the day with my first, or even second, attempt. As far as I'm concerned, one surefire path to failure is to accept mediocrity or the status quo. Something that is great today can slip to inferior quickly. The best ideas need to be fully utilized or constantly expanded in order to take them to a higher level.

11

Lesson #11:
Always Be Prepared
with Plan B . . . And
Sometimes C and D

FEAR OF FAILURE or FOF—which I referenced earlier—must be a constant sensation for any entrepreneur. In appropriate doses, FOF can provide an adrenalin boost when it is needed most. However, it can also become a way of doing business. The trick is to control FOF and not let it control you. When you do this right, an added benefit is the inherent need to stay one step ahead of the competition and remain aware of what the customer wants before he or she realizes it. It even also means being one step ahead of a problem that, if not avoided, could have become painful—or worse.

When channeled correctly, FOF transforms into a healthy respect for failure that can become one's secret sauce. It evolves into a discipline that leads to having a myriad of contingency plans—A, B, C, and, sometimes, D—for when things don't go the way you expect. In business, that's the case more often than not.

Like it or not, nobody really cares about your Plan A. You might consider your initial plan to be gospel because you slaved over it, but your customers care only about answering one question: What's in it for them? What does this do to make their lives easier, more enjoyable, and more productive? Beyond that, your plan is really only a means to an end. So, you'd better have plans B, C, and D in your back pocket for when the inevitable happens.

In the fall of 2008, when the Great "Soft" Depression hit with a vengeance, many company owners and operators started running for the hills or hunkering down in hopes of surviving the storm. Max-Wellness began in September, at just about the same time as the market started to tank. Real estate values worldwide collapsed quickly, and corporations began dropping like flies. Availability of capital almost instantly dried up. Not only were banks not lending, but many were even in danger of folding themselves, and some actually did.

To make matters worse, the supply chain began to splinter as business-to-business customers started having trouble paying their bills. Vendors were going out of business because they were caught in the credit crunch. Consumers were clutching what was left of their cash. Panic and uncertainty became the currency of the moment. This could not have occurred at a worse time for Max-Wellness.

However—as the past has proven—bad times can also be good. The trick for an entrepreneur is to figure out how to minimize the pain during difficult periods, and then maximize the opportunity that the problem presents. This economic collapse presented some unique challenges to Max-Wellness, the least of which was the unknown.

For that reason, I decided to call a time-out in October 2008. As good as you think you are, no one operates in a vacuum—and I realized I had to take a step back and ask myself some questions, many of which had no easy answer. The only thing that was clear to me was that it was time for Plan B, and maybe even fall-back plans C, D, and E.

First, I had to determine whether we should even proceed in light of the possible economic tsunami that so many doom-and-gloom prognosticators were expecting. It was clear the world was in the midst of a financial wake-up call that could not be ignored. This was the classic below-the-belt hit that precipitated cold sweats and shortness of breath. Markets, consumers, and politicians were truly gripped by fear.

We also wondered whether we should change our timetable if we did proceed—and where we were going to find enough money to roll out the concept when potential investors had almost instantly lost 25 to 50 percent of their net worth. It didn't help that both venture capital funds and private equity firms were virtually upside down with many of their portfolio companies.

Despite the fact that I don't always follow their advice, I always test the waters by talking with smart people I trust. I conferred with a few close advisers whom I quickly realized didn't know any more than I did. The most frequent response I received during the market's downward spiral was: Why are you starting a new cash-hungry business in these uncharted waters?

Yet I refused to see things through that lens. Despite the obvious peril involved with the world economy, I knew the wheels would continue to turn. People still needed goods and services, and we weren't going to revert to the preindustrial age any time soon. I quickly determined that this tsunami just might provide a number of economic opportunities. And if Max-Wellness was one of the few new retailers moving forward, we were actually in a prime position.

My best guess based on experience and a strong gut feeling was that we could create a bidding match with landlords and suppliers—which had seen their opportunities for new business dry up and were watching their existing business relationships weaken across the board. I gathered as much information as possible, identified all the issues I could imagine, put everything down in writing—and then sketched out a possible solution. Suddenly, I had a new Plan B.

As the leaves were falling from the trees, the first two full-time Max-Wellness management positions had been filled. We were officially up and running. I continued to analyze Plan B and knew it was not time to head toward the exits. But we definitely needed to hunker down, wait, watch, and listen. Something had to give soon.

The first thing I did was figure out how to stretch the financial resources we had. I slowed our management team's development. Instead of following our initial plan and moving into new, larger offices at the end of 2008, we extended the lease in our existing facilities on a month-to-month basis. It was a crowded and inconvenient environment, but at least it didn't require a major lease commitment or additional capital, which made good short-term business sense.

Next, I thought about how to secure new capital. The rules of engagement had suddenly changed, as there was no economic security anywhere. I could fund a portion of Max-Wellness with my personal resources, but not on the broad scale I knew that we needed to move forward. My original financing targets—friends, family, and affiliates—were in the same situation as everyone else, and were no longer realistic sources of capital. Nor was the private equity market, where I could have turned to numerous associates or firms had the economy been in better shape. So instead, I sought new ways to fund a business using less-than-orthodox methods.

I looked at the notes I had sketched out a few weeks earlier when the troubles began, and realized that the same factors made it a good time to move forward. It was as simple as asking one question: Who would be successful if *I* were successful? The obvious answer was landlords, developers, and suppliers.

Real estate shopping center developers were clearly in a pickle, as they had too much property and not enough tenants. Some of their publicly owned company tenants were in dire financial trouble and going down the drain rapidly. So my concept for Plan C was simple: I needed time and real estate developers' money in order to gain momentum and get Max-Wellness moving again. They needed tenants. I understood that an empty storefront is essentially a wasting asset each day it stays empty. It is the same situation as an airplane that takes off with unfilled seats; *some* revenue is always better than nothing even if the seat price has to be drastically cut to fill it.

So, what if I could make a deal with developers and landlords that would allow me to avoid paying both rent for a protracted period of time, as well as up-front cash for the store construction build-out? Securing free rent—at least for a while—would preserve existing capital, which could be used to build a scalable infrastructure.

And just like that, Plan C and the "PPP" were born.

PPP was the designation for what has come to be known as the Max-Wellness Preferred Partner Program. Instead of paying rent, these landlords and developers became investors in Max-Wellness and had a stake in its success. This program allows landlords to pay for the build-out and provide six months of free rent. Then for the next year, we would give landlords warrants to purchase equity in Max-Wellness at the same price as when we launched our first private equity institutional investment round.

The kicker was that I needed to give these PPP investors a significant bonus. For every $1 deferred in rent, the landlord would receive $1.25 in equity or a 25 percent bonus. I prepared a simple matrix that showed the economic upside of what a warrant could be worth when Max-Wellness repeated something close to what happened with OfficeMax. The simple math was that $225,000 in deferred rent could amount to several million dollars in the years ahead, when the company realized a capital event such as a recapitalization or an equity sale to a strategic player. The landlord would receive a bonus with the appreciation in the value of its equity.

My next step was to prepare a PowerPoint presentation and approach several developers. I relied on my career-long axiom: If you don't ask, you'll never get.

Although I wasn't surprised, I was pleased that these developers "got" the concept from the get-go. This should not have been too startling because more so than most others, developers understand the leverage game.

My own people, on the other hand, greeted the PPP effort with a great deal of skepticism. This again spurred me on, probably in some respects just for the sport of it.

The pitch to landlords worked well and buoyed me to jump to Step 2. I assumed that if it worked on one group, it would work on others. I'd identified vendors and suppliers that I could bring into the bidding on beneficial terms because of the economy. Plan C turned landlords into our stalking horse investor-champions. Why not expand the plan to include the other groups?

So I went to high-cost service providers and offered them the opportunity to participate in the PPP. My approach was that I was doing *them* the favor, not vice versa. I explained that our success would be their success, and that by working together, we could all make money and enjoy the journey.

I went out of my way to issue a number of disclaimers every time I made the PPP proposal. I stated that my past performance with OfficeMax was no guarantee of future success for Max-Wellness, but also explained that I did it before, and thought that I could do it again.

Within several weeks, the capital crunch that could have shelved Max-Wellness was over. Not only had we cracked the code as to how to help fund the business, but we had also developed a funding vehicle that we could employ to forge ahead with our plan. All of this was possible because we understood the importance of turning to plans B, C, and, when necessary, D.

12

Lesson #12:
You'll Never Reach Critical
Goals without a
Definitive Timetable

EVEN THE CRAFTIEST plan doesn't have a snowball's chance of succeeding unless an agenda is set that lays out when you will reach specific objectives, and concrete metrics that measure your progress. You need to be a disciplined zealot in order to create a definitive schedule like this. I am always amazed by how many companies and executives don't know how to build or use a timetable that charts critical benchmarks. Would you ever decide to embark on a trip without knowing where you were going, and determining when you might get there?

Timetables are critical for every aspect in a business. They must have meat on their bones. A functional timetable can spell the difference between just treading water and moving ahead toward a goal. Not only must they contain dates and waypoints that chronicle every major step of your journey, but they also need to factor in accountability by including who is responsible for what tasks and by when. A structure like this can—and probably will—change, as dictated by plans B, C, and D. However, you always need to have one—or you'll never be able to chart where your start-up stands on its way to becoming a functioning business.

The early days of OfficeMax found my teammates and me in full-court-press mode—not only in terms of work output, but also in hours we devoted to the cause. We had a timetable with specifics in place that I was committed to meeting. We had the attitude that the clock had no hands, which meant we were done at night only once we had accomplished the objectives assigned for that day. This meant countless days that started at 7 AM and finished at 9 PM, 10 PM, and even midnight. We worked at a pace not for the timid or meek of heart, one that certainly required a commitment from every participant's significant other. Even worse, our typical workweek had six days. Sunday became the catch-up day during which we rejuvenated; however, we also spent it mapping out our plan, checking our objectives, and updating the timetable for the next week. I spent my Sundays on outings with my wife that included visiting other retailers.

From April 1 to July 3, 1988, the initial OfficeMax team worked flat-out at full speed. My biggest fear was that people would redline and simply burn out before we got to the starting gate, which was to open the first store on July 5, 1988. That was the critical date in our initial timeline: launch day.

Subsequent to our success, many people marveled that we could build an entire organization, develop a comprehensive merchandise assortment, craft a marketing plan, and staff a back office to run a nascent retail business in a mere 90 days. Much like being a soldier in a war, it is much more fun to talk about the battle after the war is won. During the battle, you're just hoping to survive.

The reality was that we moved with such great alacrity because we had no choice. We had limited available capital available at the beginning. By my calculations, if we didn't open in early July, we ran the risk of fizzling like a bad Fourth of July fireworks display. So really, the only alternatives were to follow our timetable religiously, chase our landmarks like zealots, and ensure that we never wavered in getting off the dime. To have stopped, even for a moment, could have spelled the end before we ever began.

One of the biggest challenges during those first three months was to make sure that the original associates who started with me were always on the same page. I needed to know that they spent every minute of every day focused on the tasks needing attention. To that end, I developed a simple procedure to ensure that no one got off the path and began hitting the rocks. We could not afford either the damage or the delays.

Every morning a small group of us gathered in the confer-ence room with a blackboard, on which we would list, in numerical order, each objective for the day and who was responsible for making it happen. We would then reconvene as a group at the end of each day and check off those items that were satisfactorily completed. Those that weren't completed were transferred to another blackboard and listed as objectives for the following day.

Our approach wasn't just moving items from day to day; that is, we didn't just list the item again to list it. Instead, we focused on brainstorming a different approach to solving the specific problem that had not been solved. In this manner, we developed a movable, constantly evolving timetable.

Interestingly, we often found that we would follow a similar tack to solve those problems we hadn't solved on the previous day. However, we would do so with a slightly different twist or spin and, certainly, with more heart.

13

Lesson #13:
Never Be as Weak as Your
Weakest Link

ONE OF THE most important lessons learned in building anything is how to recognize that all the various pieces become the sum of a business. You inevitably realize that sometimes a couple of those pieces spoil under the bright lights of attention. Everything you've achieved up until this point will become immaterial if you fail to understand this lesson.

Successful entrepreneurs don't panic when parts begin to spoil. Instead, the entrepreneur asks whether those components still add real value to the equation. If they don't, the entrepreneur must be ready to do something about it. That sometimes means shifting things around, or even eliminating the piece. When it involves people, it may mean combining two functions under one person.

Too many entrepreneurs are willing to stand by and watch components deteriorate, despite the old tenet that a business is only as strong as its weakest link. They expect the stronger links to pick up the slack from the weaker ones.

However, I developed a specific mind-set for dealing with weak links many years ago. When something does not work—and if one or two fixes don't rectify the problem—I begin to look at the issue from a different perspective. The key is not assuming any part of the current setup is untouchable or sacred. Entrepreneurs must decide that what was originally envisioned as a strong component of the business just isn't happening or is not going to happen. It might be that the economics don't work; the effort to make it work isn't worth the return; or you simply conclude that you don't need that component or person to make the venture succeed.

For example, our original plan with Max-Wellness included a full-service pharmacy. As we began to determine the necessary steps, the amount of money involved, and the competition that we would encounter from national drugstore chains, I realized how problematic this would be. I concluded that the return wasn't what we needed, and that we could do a workaround by removing this component completely. We could then use the space, money, and effort on another segment of the business that would ultimately be more profitable and enhance the overall Max-Wellness concept.

Many entrepreneurs might have fallen in love with the idea of having a pharmacy in a wellness store, and pursued the pharmacy despite what the research told them. But, as a self-proclaimed realist, I try never to pick on anyone or anything my own size—and challenging someone bigger is even worse. What is equally if not more important: I am very, very circumspect about going into battle with competitors with deeper pockets than mine, as doing so would cause my odds of prevailing to deteriorate quickly. Instead, I am constantly on the lookout for workarounds.

So I took a step back, reviewed the lay of the land, and asked myself one question: Who in their right mind would knowingly take a start-up into direct, hand-to-hand combat with the likes of Walgreens, CVS, Rite Aid, and huge supermarket chains with pharmacies?

We then analyzed the situation and reviewed our overall strategy—to position ourselves as the distinctive and unique purveyor of wellness products, for enhancement of one's life, prevention of illness, and treatment of health issues. Nowhere in that strategy did it proclaim that we needed people to perceive us as a pharmacy. And even if we thought we did, the perception would not necessarily have been a positive one. For one thing, we would have been smaller than our competitors. We would not have been able to compete with their prices, especially with some chains giving away basic antibiotics and other similar drugs to entice customers into their stores. It's tough to translate "free" into a profit in any business, especially a start-up. So we determined that a pharmacy would have been a critical weak link in our plan and needed to be eliminated.

At the same time, I identified another weak link that required attention. The original structure I had created with my start-up investment partner needed tweaking. As Max-Wellness moved along, I had come to realize that we would need millions of dollars more in the first year than we had originally projected, followed by another big slug of equity money about a year and a half after that. Thus, we needed to convene and rethink our financial arrangement.

I met with my partner to discuss the situation. In order to proceed successfully, I explained, I first needed to become the majority stockholder to justify the amount of time and energy it had become apparent I would have to invest in the company. Second, we needed to bring in a significant amount of new money. And third, he was going to be diluted down to the minority position.

It took less than a week to secure the revised structure and get a new deal done. My partner was diluted down to a minority position; I became the majority owner and assumed almost sole responsibility for raising new money so that we could reach the starting blocks of opening the first stores.

14

Lesson #14:
Raising Additional Capital
Requires Creating Demand

THE KEY TO raising capital during the start-up phase is finding your stalking horse. However, once you've reached Phase Two and are developing your idea, the rules—and your needs—change. At this point, you've presumably already bought into and begun exploiting the Law of OPM. You are stretching every dollar as far as it can go, and then a little farther. But inevitably, you will need more money. And when that time comes, your next challenge is convincing people to put their chips on your table.

At its core, raising money is about creating demand. Most start-up entrepreneurs don't realize this, so they end up giving away much more than is necessary to entice investors. Think about it like the stock market: You don't buy a stock at $10 a share because you think it's going to remain at $10 a share. You buy the stock because you think its value will rise to $15, $20, or even $30 a share. People don't invest in what *is*; they invest in what *may be*. Accept this critical realization as the Holy Grail for raising money. It relies on convincing people that your idea has merit, it will work, and they can be part of a select group of early investors who will split that pot of gold at the end of the rainbow.

If you are lucky enough to grow your business to the point where you can take it public, you'll find that there is a person working for the lead underwriter on the syndicate desk called a *book runner*. This person has taken the concept of creating demand and made it an art form. In actuality, a book runner is nothing more than the person whose job it is to communicate scarcity. He works the phone, calling the mutual funds and saying, "Guys, hey, I've got Mike Feuer coming to town and his company OfficeMax is doing an initial public offering (IPO). First indications are that it's a hot deal and we can probably get you some stock, but there's not going to be enough to give you what you'll want. However, we'll get you in because we have a long-term relationship."

Raising money is really just about supply and demand. There's a theory that I haven't quite fleshed out completely but am working on to this day, and it goes a bit like this: Owners think that their competitors are 10 times smarter and savvier than they really are. To combat this idea you must create an impression that you are that guy with the answers. This takes a certain smugness that almost borders on a sort of benevolent arrogance. It also requires good presentation and acting skills. Finally, you need the ability to generate demand in the market-place for whatever it is you're peddling.

I realize that not everybody can do this, and although I'm not yet sure what the proper combination of the key factors really is, I have come to this conclusion: If you make it so easy to get that everyone could invest in something during the start-up and build-out phases, why would anyone want to invest? Moreover, even if they would, why would they pay you what you want them to pay for the opportunity?

I've worked hard to take this theory to a certain level in my own applications. I helped create demand for Max-Wellness by creating news. In November 2008 I made a phone call to the Cleveland newspaper the *Plain Dealer* and told them I was planning to do an interview with a major national media service about my plans to open the next great retail chain. I told the *Plain Dealer* reporter that I would be launching my next business in Cleveland, and added that because the city had been good to me (which was certainly true) and OfficeMax over the years, the paper could have the story about Max-Wellness first—if it moved quickly. There was, however, one caveat: They had only four days from the time of the interview to publish the story before I began doing interviews with other media outlets.

Suddenly, I had a big story on the front page of the business section of the *Plain Dealer* that turned out to be one of my best stories ever.

My time at OfficeMax taught me a lot about the inner workings of the media. They, too, are in the business of "demand"; after all, journalists have to worry about whether they're going to be scooped by other reporters. Editors worry about whether their competitors are going to break a good story first. Understanding these factors can help you get the necessary forces working together for you and your business. The press you generate allows you to craft your story the way you want it to be told. And when you're raising money, it helps to create that feeling of "something special" that produces demand. It's like the old example of the girl who's much more attractive on the other guy's arm; when you create scarcity, everybody wants to get in on the party.

Another key to getting media coverage is to use the kind of "rifle approach" I cited earlier. Rather than send out a news release to dozens of publications in hopes that they will pick it up, try to develop a credible initial relationship with one reporter. Keep in mind that what you have to say must first and foremost be news and fact-based. Reporters are smart and they won't be played. You must give them something in order to get something in return.

Try to become a source for reporters by offering to be their behind-the-scenes specialist in your area of expertise. Consider helping the reporter with a story that doesn't even mention your business. This can pay dividends down the road in a number of ways, including being the first person the reporter contacts when working on a new story that might tie to your company.

Reporters can also be a good source of information because they are always talking to people on their respective beats. Reporters have a good sense of what's going on and who's involved. Over the years I've made good friends with many journalists. I've found that they are much like entrepreneurs because they find ingenious ways of creating their own types of supply and demand.

With those pieces in place you then have to figure out your pitch and to whom you'll make it. I've learned throughout my career that most people panic when they recognize that they have to ask for money from others when all they have is a concept or when they've tapped the initial round of cash they fought so hard to raise in the first place. Asking is much more difficult than getting; however, it becomes much easier if you can learn how to make a strong presentation and tell your story.

Attention, interest, desire, and action are the key elements of selling. To start the process, you must not bore people. I knew within five minutes of approaching (or being approached by) an investor for money whether I had a shot of selling them. Think about your "elevator pitch" when telling your story: A guy gets in the elevator with you on the 15th floor. You know that before the chime sounds indicating you've reached the lobby, you have to be able to explain the who, what, where, when, why, and how of your idea. You must get him to understand the concept and be interested enough to think seriously about investing with you before he leaves the elevator.

Without a doubt, the number-one skill needed in raising money is the ability to craft a succinct, compelling story that won't put the potential investor to sleep. You need to be able to weave in an appropriate dose of drama and sell investors not on what you have today, but on what it will be tomorrow. After that, you need to wow them with a scenario of how and when they get to a payday, as well as the kind of realistic return on investment they can expect. And you have to do all of this without making promises you can't keep, and while explaining the potential risks.

It all comes down to good communications with a flair that causes investors to buy into your dream. It's worth repeating: You are allowed to do almost anything during that sales pitch except bore the prospects. Bore them and you're dead in the water before you ever see that first dime.

Once you have your pitch down pat, you need to approach a broad-enough group of individual investors so that you spread the potential controlling interests around. Rarely do you find a single person who says, "Okay. How much?" and then writes a check to cover all your needs. And even when that does happen, you should ask yourself whether you want one investor with too much clout.

Title : The man of numbers :
Author : Devlin, Keith J.
Item ID: 30112103774136
Due   : 11/12/2011

Title : The benevolent dictator :
Author : Feuer, Michael J.
Item ID: 30112103780661
Due   : 11/12/2011

Title : Franklin and Eleanor :
Author : Rowley, Hazel
Item ID: 30112103557150
Due   : 11/12/2011

Title : No ordinary time :
Author : Goodwin, Doris Kearns.
Item ID: 30112101893359
Due   : 11/12/2011

During my second round with Max-Wellness, I developed a target list of potential investors with strict criteria. First, I wanted passive new money to come in. Second, I wanted investors who could play in a high-stakes game without being ruined if things did not work out as planned. I've always believed in full disclosure, and that you can ask for or tell just about anything as long as you do so honestly and spell out the good, the bad, and the ugly. And that's exactly what we did in developing our second-round private placement strategy.

I knew that I did not want professional institutional investors in this round. I made this determination because—given the 2008 economic meltdown—I would have to jump through too many hoops to get the money from traditional private equity or venture funds. Although I probably could have done it, it would have taken too much of my time, particularly without stores up and running. Additionally, professional money had more than its own share of trouble at this time. I reasoned that once we had the first stores up, operating, and successful, new money would find us.

Although I do not believe that "If you build it, they will come," I do believe that people will find you if you package what you do in the appropriate light and shine a spotlight on your accomplishment. Another way of saying this: The best way to attract the desired party(ies) is to stand still and let that person or group come to you, but first you must create the appropriate environment for that to happen.

Accordingly, I approached several people who had a reputation for taking a calculated risk for round-two financing. I did not know some of these people well, and although others were not OfficeMax investors, they had bemoaned that fact every time I had seen them over the past 20 years. So I made a few phone calls, explained the Max-Wellness story along with why we were raising another round of capital, and asked if that investor had any interest. We managed—without a great deal of effort—to quickly generate the next round of capital.

I cited hypothetical, yet documented, valuations that I had previously achieved during my presentation to the second-round investors. I explained what a successful deal might produce, and also pointed out that building a business is like traveling through a minefield—there are bound to be a few small explosions, but the big fear is that game-ending blast. I ended by telling them that they should invest in a start-up only if they had the proverbial "mad money" to make the—albeit very good—bet.

Back when I was launching OfficeMax, we sold interests at $50 per share in the first round of capital generation. We raised the price to $87.50 for the second round, even though we didn't have much going yet other than the fact that we had kept our promise and opened the first three stores. We based the price on the notion that we'd done the research and formulated the plan. We had functional prototypes—a laboratory, if you will—in which we could continue to explore and develop our concept.

By the time I was launching Max-Wellness, I'd learned a lot about deal making and financial structure. The beauty of the free enterprise system's architecture is that you can make up the rules as you go along—provided the other side agrees and there is full transparency and disclosure. For that reason, I believe that this truly is a wonderful country.

The initial capitalization for Max-Wellness was $2 million, which gave the company an enterprise value of $2 million. I arbitrarily crafted a plan to raise additional money, which dictated that post-money basis—the enterprise value of the entity after new money was brought—would be worth $8.5 million. And that was before I even opened the first store.

There was nothing inappropriate about this step up in value. We had spent the prior 10 months developing our strategy, merchandise plan, store design, and operating management team. We were now ready to open stores and become an operating company. We had a plan and structure that we felt would work instead of just an idea. This structure was also an excellent vehicle to use to raise additional capital so that we could open our first four stores.

I also had an "aha" moment as we began to raise capital for Max-Wellness. I came to the realization in thinking through the investment that I should "invest in what I know best." As the second round of financing was ending, I decided to make a substantial investment in Max-Wellness rather than use just other people's money. I plunked down seven figures in second-round financing and made my big bet—on my team and myself. My wife Ellen—always my staunchest supporter and a successful original OfficeMax investor—decided without any prodding from me to use her own money for an investment in Max-Wellness as well.

One of the hardest things for an entrepreneur to accept is that you will never be done raising money, even after your organization is a success. No matter the level of demand you create or the number of people you have interested in investing, most if not all cases will require you to get more investors and more fresh capital. The journey essentially becomes your life.

15

Lesson #15:
Everything You Wanted to
Know about the "D" Word
but Were Afraid to Ask

MOST ENTREPRENEURS HATE the "D" word—as in *dilution*—but dilution is not a negative in my vocabulary. This term refers to the percent of ownership one gives up when selling new shares or units to another investor. Here's an example: Let's say you own 1,000 shares valued at $1 each, which represent 100 percent of the business. If you then sell 500 more shares to raise money to grow, you would be diluted by 50 percent, even though you still have the same 1,000 shares.

The only question that matters when it comes to dilution is whether you would rather have a smaller piece of a big pie or a bigger piece of a tiny pie. An entrepreneur is almost always much better off with the former. I've found it best to find ways to keep control even though I wasn't the largest investor. This is particularly true when you become a major enterprise with institutional investors.

I was petrified of the D word when I began OfficeMax, and guarded my equity in the business like a hawk. I was afraid to add more ownership, because I knew it would decrease my—and other existing investors'—shares in the company. However, this concern didn't last long; I quickly came to my senses and realized that there was no way I could build a business of any significance without OPM. First of all, I just didn't have enough money of my own. Second, I needed others to share my risk by contributing money instead of leveraging everything I owned to generate enough capital. Third, I needed to give a team equity—or "skin in the game"—to commit and do whatever it took to get the job done. I had to make it so that my success was the team's success, too. Finally, I realized that if I were the sole big owner, there was no way other people would want to work so hard to make me rich—especially when they were working for ordinary salaries during the difficult startup phase.

This revelation led me to use a simple method for getting employees engaged—the notion of ownership. First, they deserved it. Second, I needed people who I knew had my own and the company's back 24/7. I had to be sure that they were always thinking about what their actions would cost the business if they were not paying attention and made dumb mistakes.

Essentially, if an employee went above and beyond, then giving him or her equity was a small price to pay. Giving equity causes your employees to begin subscribing to the "3 AM syndrome," which means that you won't be the only one awake in the middle of the night staring at the ceiling, trying to find elusive answers to sticky problems. By becoming partners, your employees share your pain—and therefore certainly deserve to share the gain as well.

For this reason, we decided to give every employee "founder's stock" in the first few weeks of OfficeMax. This meant giving them stock out of my own and my then-partner's own pockets in exchange for their efforts. From day one, we gave store management equity, too.

Presenting the plan for this type of effort requires a high degree of creativity and ingenuity. When you have absolutely nothing in the business's early stages and you've yet to create value, merely telling people that you're going to share your nothing with them is not particularly motivating. On the other hand, when you have an idea and can articulate your dream in such a way that you're able to explain where you believe the company will be in one or two years, then whoever is listening can start to anticipate the potential rewards.

The next step is to methodically translate any hypothetical situations into examples of what one's share might be worth in 12, 24, and 36 months. I am proud of the fact that most of OfficeMax's initial employees reached financial success that they would have otherwise never imagined. Many became almost significantly wealthier than they had ever dreamed. When I sold the company, many employees made millions, and a great number made hundreds of thousands of dollars. One of the most gratifying aspects of building a big company comes with knowing that those who worked with you experienced a life-altering change—both experiential and financial.

An interesting phenomenon evolved as I made equity awards: The equity that I gave others skyrocketed in value, and lo and behold, my own equity increased in value along with that of the people who received the stock. I was literally blown away by the amount of money that I made in the first couple of years of

OfficeMax simply by sharing both my wealth and responsibility. The more I gave to others on the team, the more I benefited.

Before you get carried away, one thing you definitely do *not* want to do is give someone an immediate home run just because they're still breathing and in the right place at the right time. There must always be safeguards in place. The incentive programs that we created provided vesting schedules, which rewarded the recipient on an ongoing basis over a specified period of time, usually five years.

Max-Wellness investors earn equity in the form of profit units, which are similar to stock. Our typical vesting schedule would give a holder 40 percent of his grant of stock or profit units after 24 months. We then add another 20 percent each year for the ensuing three years until an employee is 100 percent vested. Once vested, equity cannot be taken away from the recipient unless he commits an act that is detrimental to the company— typically defined as stealing, any other type of fraud, or anti-company activities. Other than that, as long as recipients put in the time and work, they receive the equity.

The advantage of this structure is that an employee has to stick around for at least the critical first two years in order to make real money. We do not give more before that time because it takes at least a year for someone to produce anything of true value—we need to find people who are in it for the long haul.

I have actually improved the employee equity program at Max-Wellness by converting from awarding stock options (that can be exercised at a given price) to giving outright profit units in the company at no cost to the grantee. When the company reaches a capital event or milestone—be it a change of control, such as selling out or selling a large piece of the company, recapitalizing the business, or an initial public offering (IPO)— the vesting timetable accelerates. Those with options or units then reach the "cha-ching" point and ring the bell, putting money in their own pockets.

Vesting schedules can be an unpopular concept with employees in big corporations, because they must stick around and produce for the prescribed length of time in the vesting schedule. In many large companies there are also a number of forfeiture provisions; for example, if the employee jumps to a competitor (which could actually be named in the option agreement). My view is that people should be paid to play, but never get a free lunch. However, this is a surefire way to create golden handcuffs with sticking power for a smaller or privately held company.

16

Lesson #16:
Managing People Is
about Achieving Objectives
through Others

ANY TIME YOU put more than two people together in the same room, you're going to run into politics and a variety of human-resource–type issues—which usually creates problems and distractions. However, you'll sleep a little easier if you remember this one thing: Managing people is nothing more than achieving specific objectives through others. Sometimes you simply have to show, coach, or teach them how to do it. And other times, you must tell them to get over it and, as the Nike slogan proclaims, they need to "just do it."

Entrepreneurs commonly fail in the early stages because they think they can do everything themselves. What's worse is that even when they realize they can't, they don't recognize what things they should be hiring others to handle and which tasks they should be performing themselves.

Not surprisingly, many entrepreneurs tend to do the things they like and think they can do better than anyone themselves. They don't take the time to teach others how to complete these tasks and therefore free themselves to tackle more substantive issues and opportunities that provide a bigger payback. In situations like these, entrepreneurs are ultimately doomed to fail or run out of steam, because they are constantly exhausted. This also usually means that some critical must-do items never get done.

There is a geometric progression in business: As your venture gets more complex, your day becomes more compressed. You are then more likely to run out of time before you accomplish what has to be done. Additionally, there's always a quality-of-life issue lurking just over the horizon.

Nowadays, I start my work with Max-Wellness at about 7:30 AM from home—writing and answering e-mail, outlining next steps, and making calls. I intentionally don't show up at the office until about 10 AM because I don't want to be too available. I don't want my executive team coming to me with problems that they should be able to handle just because I happen to be there. In fact, I should be the *last* stop they make when they hit an initial dead end. This requires teaching others to do what I do well and pointing them in the right direction—which is also the first step in the new entrepreneur learning to delegate.

Unfortunately, most entrepreneurs don't do a great job of delegating. Some fail because they don't know how; others don't have the time; still others are reluctant to pass the baton. The things the entrepreneur does well become his or her security blanket. But once you start hiring people to manage aspects of your business and help take it to where you want it to go, you need to learn how to become an effective teacher and mentor. For example, some of the best doctors I know are accomplished teachers who learned to leverage their knowledge for the greater good. It is no different with a CEO—whether you're heading an early-stage business or a Fortune 500 company.

Teaching is an art unto itself. In most cases, you can teach by example—by showing, by pointing, and by helping people "get it." The issue that most people have with teaching is time. You have to invest your time to train others to do it the right way. Although it can be painful at first, there is a huge payback if you persevere—in terms of both increased productivity to your business and the satisfaction you obtain by passing your talent on to others. Medical schools and hospitals have a method for training new docs who will eventually train others: "Watch one, do one, teach one."

You also have to keep people off the rocks. Think of it like this: An employee is traveling down a narrow road with many rocks along the sides. He or she veers off the road and hits the rocks. The employee gets hurt and damage is done. Your job as the leader is to keep people going safely down the path and off the rocks so they can get where you want them to with minimal damage and pain. Although it seems simple, many entrepreneurs don't understand this until they've been in a few collisions with immovable objects and near-death experiences.

Another critical element to managing people is carefully choosing pronouns. Business today needs more "we" and less "me." When I was consulting companies between retail gigs, it would make me crazy when seasoned executives and would-be entrepreneurs started running off at the mouth with litanies of "I," "I," and "I." I could tell within 10 minutes what kind of leader someone was by his or her choice of pronouns. Changing the pronouns you use allows you to transform yourself into the type of leader people want to follow—and, in the process, you'll become a better teacher.

My rule at OfficeMax was that if something bad happened, "I" did it—as far as the outside world was concerned. But when things were great, it was always "we." Following this rule lets you build a fully committed team that will follow you anywhere. I was able to shoulder the blame in public when things went south simply by using the pronoun "I." It also seems eminently fair that because I owned the most stock and made the most money that I should take the most heat. And most of the time, I probably deserved the grief anyway.

Using pronouns properly also provides the latitude you need as CEO to take people kicking and screaming over the finish line. The right pronoun—as in "we"—will help employees realize that they are accountable. It helps them see that the company will sink or swim because of the team, not just the lead player.

Interestingly, I never once thought OfficeMax would fail. I also never thought that we weren't going to make this company big—despite the fact that we had numerous, extremely well-funded competitors before we even opened our first store. Because I made my opinions apparent, my mind-set became viral, and people bought into my beliefs—mostly because I really, truly was convinced of them myself, and knew how to sell them—despite my few dark moments.

I have always thought that success is usually just a matter of how painful and costly it will be to win. I'm not a Pollyanna by any means; I just am a believer. I don't fixate on the downside. Instead, I focus my attention on how to achieve the upside and then some. To that end, we hired many people in the early OfficeMax days with the same mind-set and positive attitude. They were focused on reaching the upside, no matter what it took.

On April 1, 1988, the first official day of the start of OfficeMax, I arrived at work dressed in my best blue suit, white shirt, and red tie. Everybody else showed up in jeans, wrinkled khakis, flip-flops, and casual garb that I wouldn't wear to take out the garbage.

Business has a lot of do with creating the right image and using theatrics to get the message across. At that time, our company had no money. We hadn't even closed on our first capital raise yet. In addition, nobody knew anything about how exactly we intended to turn this idea into a national retail chain. Despite that fact, I had woken up that first day and said to myself, "It's showtime. At least look like you fit the part." My appearance was my attempt to show my employees what I thought a successful company looks like and how it presents itself to the outside world.

My team quickly got the message. By the end of that first week, every single person came in to work dressed the part— men in a tie and jacket, women in skirts or pantsuits. For about the next 10 years, we never had another casual day. I used that image as a marketing tool and carried that presentation into the OfficeMax stores as well. We were selling to business professionals in our stores and we had to look professional, too.

One of the most difficult lessons I learned about managing people is that it is imperative to have an evolving team. The cold reality of the pure start-up is that the entrepreneur must know that the people who began with him or her most likely won't be finishing in the same role where they started. The stark fact is that a start-up works for people at certain times in their lives. A key rule to my own hiring is that I always try to recruit somebody who has something to prove to him- or herself, and usually somebody else as well. A savvy entrepreneur needs to know how to push those buttons and put people in a position where they can rise to the occasion and excel. Doing so compels them to achieve the entrepreneur's objectives and satisfy their own personal and occasionally deep-seated needs.

Another reality is that when the enterprise begins to accelerate exponentially—particularly as it did with OfficeMax—there is not always enough time to take the person holding the job initially to the next level of management. That means bringing in someone with more experience to replace that person. The good news here is that the entrepreneur doesn't have to throw the person who's currently holding the job under the bus. Instead, candor is the best antidote to deal with this inevitability of growth. I told my new employees that they could go further faster at OfficeMax than anywhere else at that point in their lives. However, I also let them know that there may come a time when, through no fault of their own, they may not be able to get to the next level.

I had many successful examples in which good, solid workers made a lot of money with me in the start-up phase of OfficeMax. While they continued to do so for many years thereafter, they often held jobs that were one, two, three, or four notches below the level they initially held. It comes down to honesty, as well as something else I found: In most cases, people know in their heart of hearts when enough is enough, and that the increased responsibility is beyond their current abilities.

One of the greatest mistakes that leaders make is that they're always looking for all long-ball hitters who will emerge as their team MVPs. Although that is an enviable goal, it is not usually realistic. You don't need A players for every position in the company; many times, B and C players do fine. For example, a top executive must be at least a B or higher player, but a receptionist can be very good as a C player if he or she has the right attitude. It gets down to matching the position and person with the need. Most businesses tend to be unrealistic about filling all their positions with overachievers, which is usually economically impractical.

There are other reasons why you can't have a team filled with superstars. If everyone on the team is an A player, you more than likely have just too much drama as each person tries to prove that his or her idea is the right way to do things. Instead, you need leaders, doers, and a good number of loyal followers. I have had many bright employees who, for whatever reason, lacked a certain skill or set of skills. This will work fine as long as you always set the bar commensurate with what needs to be done and what one has the capabilities of reaching.

I also tried to identify people who had the potential but never the opportunity to be superstars. I would always push them to go higher and establish scenarios to test them to see how they would think and what they would do under adverse circumstances. One of my favorite practices is to ask people questions for which I already know the answer. This is not much different from a teacher giving a student a test to see what they know.

I also tell people that I don't want to be their father. Instead, I let them know that I set the direction, but that they have to do their own work and mind their own troubles. Further, I explain that what they could achieve is limited only by their own creativity, imagination, and endurance.

It was also during these early days at OfficeMax that I would begin fine-tuning the concept of what *no* really means and how to overcome a negative reply, leading to a positive outcome. In essence, I began teaching my employees that no—at least the first time—really means *maybe*, primarily because the naysayer doesn't yet understand the benefits. I told them that unless someone tells you no 10 times and follows it with a slap, it isn't really *no*.

Although there is certainly humor in this promulgation, I've often found that there was more truth than fiction in the statement. Hearing *no* simply meant that we might not have effectively or passionately explained what we needed—or adequately expressed why our success would be their success.

Another lesson I constantly teach and even preach is that many a company has encountered huge problems by not sweating the small stuff. The axiom "retail is detail" says it all and applies to virtually every type of business. Almost all of my experience comes back to the fact that a leader must effectively become a master teacher in order to achieve the desired objectives through others.

17

Lesson #17:
Good Intentions Will
Get You Only So Far

HIRING AND FIELDING a team for a start-up is much like running a spring training baseball farm team. You recruit players to see what they have by putting them on the field with a bat, ball, and glove. You then attempt to see if the players have the right stuff, or at least some talent that can be nurtured. It doesn't take long to figure out who is going to make it and who won't, no matter how hard they might try.

After a few months of bringing some rookies and one key merchant onto the Max-Wellness team, I had a fairly good idea of their capabilities. Unfortunately, the game rules were changing while I was doing this, due to the dramatically deteriorating economic environment. I realized that it was no longer business as usual. Some of the tactics I had used and that worked 20 years earlier were, in some instances, no longer applicable in this new world order of survival of the fittest. I was operating where I had never been previously, and the rules were changing rapidly.

Because I had the battle scars from 15 years of running OfficeMax from start-up to $5 billion in sales, I knew that I had to strengthen the Max-Wellness team lest I wind up doing all of the work myself. It became clear that the margin for error was razor-thin and we could not afford any significant missteps. I decided to find a few additional key executives who had the type of experience I needed and entice them to join the team.

Every entrepreneur learns this lesson and, in many cases, continues to do so as he or she builds new businesses. Simply put, there isn't a good fairy who is going to come and solve your problems. The responsibility for fixing something falls squarely on the entrepreneur's shoulders—and that takes having the right person doing the right job, the right way. It requires that you hire someone who is able to do it once and do it right.

The best way to avoid issues is to find people who have done before what you need them to do now. You want employees who've already made their mistakes and undergone the learning curve on another company's nickel. Everyone makes mistakes; the smart ones learn from the missteps so as not to make the error twice. The scary ones are the people who just chase their tails in a circle, repeating the same mistakes and never realizing why.

At the same time, I knew that the point had come when we needed to draw a definite line in the sand and establish a drop-dead date to open the first store. Since the economy started to implode, I'd been hedging on a key business principle: that in order to get from Point A to Point Z, there would be light at the end of the tunnel and, as the saying goes—the light wouldn't be from a train heading straight toward us.

I wasn't in a huge rush to pick an opening date while the economy was unraveling, because I wanted to see how far down "down" really was. Once I got the sense that the world wasn't coming to an end, it was time to put the pieces together and form a definitive timeline. I was still very concerned about business conditions, consumers' perceptions, and their attitudes toward spending money. Unfortunately, in many cases, perception is much more important than reality.

Eventually, however, one has to put up or shut up. We had raised the money and developed a definitive marketing strategy. The team needed a target, so I picked the first week in January 2010 to open the prototype Max-Wellness. It was located in the far western Cleveland suburb of Westlake.

One of the aspects of building a start-up is that before the first sale is made it is much like *A Tale of Two Cities*, because it's the best of times and the worst of times. The best is that the CEO can go to bed and not worry about whether the business made its sales target for the day. Stores not yet opened don't generate a penny of revenue. This means no sales targets or same store sales to beat.

The worst of times for me during this start-up period was that several hundred thousand dollars a month were going out, and not a penny was coming in.

Toward the end of the summer, I kept telling our team that the clock would begin ticking more loudly on the day after Labor Day. Yet they all began that Tuesday at work not really expecting anything different than they had been dealing with the week before.

Well, it wasn't as if they hadn't been warned.

First thing on that Tuesday morning, I called a series of four meetings to take place in the ensuing 24 hours with people from each major area of the business. I also established new check-points, which basically stated that we would have a senior executive committee management team meeting three times every week: one on Monday afternoons at four o'clock; a second on Wednesday at the same time; and a final one at the end of the day Friday. I informed my team that we could not afford any surprises. Everyone in management had to know what everyone else was doing; we had to make sure that one area did not adversely affect another because of a missed deadline or process or procedure.

I laid out the ground rules of how we would be operating from September until we opened the first store in January 2010. After establishing the initial, all-important "no surprises" rule, my second rule was: If the person responsible for doing something couldn't get it done, he or she had to discuss the issue at one of the three weekly all-hands status updates. This would give others the opportunity to either pitch in or determine a workaround.

Although everyone seemed a bit dazed during the first week, they proceeded at an accelerated pace. By the second week, they all "got with the program"—and the tempo reached the level I expected and the company needed. All of a sudden, people stopped e-mailing and texting each other, and instead got off their rear ends and walked over to one another to discuss the problems or opportunities they were facing. It prompted them to resolve issues at lightning speed, and it was a working lesson in the power of clear communications. We set a goal, and told everyone what the objectives were. We let them know where the finish line was in terms of when we must be open for business.

I also made one thing clear as part of my strategy to turn up the heat: Just because we had planned to do something a certain way three months ago, it didn't mean that we couldn't rework or reassess that decision today. Three months ago we thought that a particular method would work; three months later we had a clearer idea of how to approach it. This related to the notion of a plan versus a forecast. Most companies create a plan, which then becomes cast in concrete—a recipe for disaster. When a plan becomes carved in stone, it is only a matter of when—not if—it will start to crack.

Building a new business is always a work in progress—the team had better get smarter as circumstances change. I manage with what I call *plan to forecast*. This means that every month into the year we update what is really happening versus what we originally expected to happen. We spend money based on the forecast, which is our best guess at that moment. This works far better than using a plan that we usually created before the start of the year—or in the case of the start-up, when the company was launched—and that isn't changed for the ensuing 52 weeks.

There are 365 reasons why people will either have huge problems or miss great opportunities when they fail to adapt to change. Change occurs as measured in days and weeks—not months or years—more so today than ever before. You should always base business expenses—everything from payroll to capital—on the most current information and trends. When my people ask me to approve an expense that was in the original plan, I tell them I don't care about the plan—unless the results are exactly on plan, which seldom if ever happens. Instead, I tell them to show me how the expense fits with the current forecast. I also don't really care (within reason) how much someone wants to spend. What I *do* care about is how the expense will enable us to do this or that, and provide a return on the investment. If I'm asked to approve a thousand-dollar expense that doesn't have a return, the conversation is usually a short one that concludes with a two-letter-word answer. However, if the expense is a million that can give us a tenfold return, I'm all ears.

Entrepreneurs must train a team to think in terms of what kind of return on investment or ROI their expenses elicit. When done properly, people can discover some really productive ways to invest capital and measure the return to justify the expense. This is what growth and progress are all about.

I have found that in difficult times, the strong get stronger and the marginal players fall by the wayside. The good managers know how to develop methods and strategies to make every dollar go further, and even do double duty. Good intentions are important, but they will get someone to the starting gate only if they're lucky—and seldom to the finish line. I tell my team that we pay for performance, not perspiration.

18

Lesson #18:
Don't Open the Doors until the Start-Up Passes the Smell Test—And Don't Be Afraid to Call Time-Out Just to Be Sure

AS A BUSINESS develops, the original concept must endure a "shake-down" process that's a lot like taking a ship to sea for trials—one that includes fully vetting each aspect of the operation and strategy. Once you've passed this series of hurdles, the real fun and work begin. It takes much more than just pointing people in the right direction and expecting them to get there. Instead you must employ a course of checks and balances, incorporate predetermined benchmarks, and conduct smell tests.

You must be careful not to be lulled into a false sense of security by thinking that everything is fine just because you don't see the storm clouds forming. I've found that many entrepreneurs miss these potential problems because everyone tends to look in the wrong direction. You can avoid this—and continue to encourage enthusiasm—by continuously trusting but verifying. Have faith in your plans and your employees, but make sure that things are going as envisioned or as they claim. It's equally important to realize, as I've emphasized before, that not every piece will pan out as originally scripted. Often what you had thought would be a great solution falls flat or never sees the light of day after more intense scrutiny. For example, we conducted numerous smell tests for different products when we launched Max-Wellness, only to find out that some products did not fit the merchandise mix. We could not rationalize the amount of shelf space needed, or found that the economics were not favorable enough to meet our risk–reward criteria.

If left to its own devices, a start-up team might go from A to Z and spend countless amounts of time, effort, and money to accomplish a task only to find at the end of the line that it no longer makes any sense or it doesn't fit in the plans. This gets down to what I call the "don't confuse me with the facts" syndrome or turning a blind eye to reality.

As we accelerated the pace, the pieces to our puzzle began to fall into place and our optimism gained momentum. At the same time, we hit our fair share of dry holes. Things that we thought would be slam dunks turned out to be duds. Instead of bemoaning the wasted energy and time, we simply did a U-turn and went back to where we started to take another path. We kept track of every significant process and protocol with an elaborate electronic project management task list, and monitored in detail every one of the approximately 650-plus tasks necessary to open.

Our tracking process included the task, who was responsible, and when it was to be completed. We embedded checkpoints in the linear progression where another person—or the entire executive committee—would weigh in to determine if this specific item was working as planned and, sometimes, whether we should even continue to proceed with it. This is all part of the value proposition and the ongoing analysis of whether what we had undertaken had a good chance of producing as promised.

This is yet another example of reducing a number to its lowest common denominator, and ensuring that it would evoke the expected customer response. We had to be sure that the tasks we were completing were not just *nice* but *necessary*. Unless the task contributed to the end result, we had to forget it and save our time, money, and energy; we had to put precious assets toward an effort that added to our major objective.

As the new store launch was nearing the finish line, we also called periodic time-outs on certain aspects of our goals. This is much like temporarily stopping before crossing a street, and taking the time to look both ways carefully before proceeding. Sometimes taking a deep breath goes a long way toward avoiding stepping into the traffic.

I've always been skeptical about undertakings that run at full speed from the beginning to the end. These situations usually incur far too many mistakes because everybody is so exhausted that they get sloppy and worry just about getting finished, rather than the quality of the final product.

Many new start-ups—and even some more mature companies—spend the bulk of their time looking only for the finish line instead of savoring the learning experience of the journey. However, a truly successful company will never see an end. The only real end occurs when and if it goes out of business.

Otherwise, business is an ongoing metamorphosis; each change leads to a better way to serve its market and its customers while making the company more productive. One of the major themes that I keep pounding home with the Max-Wellness team is that if we do our jobs correctly and become an industry leader, we will never be satisfied, and therefore, we will never be "done."

In the initial stages of building a company, the management team certainly must focus on a task-oriented approach to achieving specific goals. It makes sense to take this approach with certain parameters, such as the length of time and the amount of money and effort invested. However, an entrepreneur can never lose sight of the big picture: to have a broad perspective view of the entire package using a wide-angle lens. This lens must have the ability to zoom in when necessary on every aspect of the business, down to the smallest details that a customer will immediately see or eventually uncover.

As the launch date for the first Max-Wellness store loomed on the horizon, we continued to tweak virtually everything within the store's four walls. I looked at everything through customers' eyes during this process, and was asking if things made sense. Did everything we had done add to their shopping experience? For example, did the signage provide appropriate information, or did it just add confusion?

Starting on Monday, November 2, 2009, I began a series of countdown messages to heighten the sense of urgency, which I titled "T-minus" messages. I e-mailed them to every company member as well as key outsiders such as our advertising agency team. It was the first thing the team would see when they checked their e-mail in the morning. These messages counted down the days and included a brief message that I thought would keep everyone focused, provide encouragement, and remind them that if any issue arose—no matter how seemingly small—they should immediately bring it the attention of everyone involved. A few examples of some of those messages are:

- "Don't keep problems a secret. It's much worse to fail to tell others who will be affected that there is a problem."
- "The pressure is certainly mounting. A good antidote to pressure is a good sense of humor."
- "We're learning new things every day. Don't fall in love with a process; fall in love with what will be produced. When you find a better way, just do it."
- "Max-Wellness is your canvas and we're working together to create a masterpiece."
- "By the end of today, you'll discover yet another opportunity on how to improve what we're doing. Keep a keen eye out for that special opportunity."

This was no time for heroics or for people to try to solve problems on their own. Though it's a bit corny, it's also true that there is no "I" in team. I diligently worked to keep everyone focused on the goal; however, I didn't want them to put on their blinders and miss the warning signs because they were moving too fast.

We also recognized that the real work would truly begin once the first store opened. All of the research, planning, and strategy meant little until the customers voted with their wallets. I was always amazed in the case of OfficeMax at how little we really knew until we launched the stores, tested the products, and experimented with new merchandise. The second the very first store opened, we began a strange "encounter of the third kind," which takes us to Phase Three: constant reinvention.

Phase Three

Constant Reinvention

19

Lesson #19:
Pot Stirring 101—The Key to
Continuous Reinvention

As a FOUNDER and former CEO of a Fortune 500 company, I have given more than 1,000 talks and speeches over the past 25 or some years. I am invariably asked the same question during each presentation's question-and-answer session: What is a CEO's most important role in an organization?

The audience doubtlessly expects a pat, textbook-type response—"building a team," "accelerating sales and profits," or "increasing shareholders' value." And all of these truly are critically important objectives, each of which provides a barometer of effectiveness and success.

However, my answer to this age-old question was—and still is—"A boss's job is to stir the pot."

I personally disdain the status quo. The trite saying "If it ain't broke, don't fix it" sets me off. The comment "Same old, same old" when applied to a business's progress is, as far as I'm concerned, the first sign that a company is heading into obscurity. Getting a start-up venture off the ground with some modicum of success can lull an entrepreneur into a dangerous mind-set where he or she begins to relax a bit and starts "smelling the roses."

One of the truly fun aspects of being a boss is that, at times, you get to make up certain rules of exploration and engagement. You establish the goals, create expectations, and determine measurements. You also get to keep thinking about better ways to do what's already working. Yet one of the biggest threats facing small, medium, and yes, even Fortune 500 companies is inertia. If you were at least half-awake in high school physics, you should know that inertia is the tendency to resist acceleration, unless disturbed by an external force. This translates in the business world to a lack of ability or desire to move an organization forward.

The boss is the individual who must act as that "external force" for continuous, systematic change and innovation. He or she must be poised to seize the moment and capitalize on unique opportunities when they're presented. Good companies, institutions, and organizations not only serve their customers' current needs, but also anticipate potential preferences that customers have yet to recognize themselves. Did the world know it needed e-mail to communicate 25 years ago? Did anyone guess 30 years ago that cell phones would become virtually ubiquitous around the world and used by hundreds of millions of consumers? I think not. But there was a leader somewhere—a pot stirrer extraordinaire—who challenged others to think about "What if?" and to improve a product, process, or procedure.

And although this tenet is imperative to maintaining an organization committed to continuous reinvention and innovation, nowhere is it more important than once you've opened the doors to your business and the cash register begins ringing. There is a tendency at the beginning of this third critical phase to focus on selling as many products as possible and growing sales—*without* considering whether what you're doing is anything more than a quick-hit fad that will taper or die off when the competition figures out a better way.

So how do you keep your organization energized, recognizing that once people are done creating they'll have to do it all over again, and then again and again?

One effective method is to have more than one team ready in the wings to begin working on the same product or project. When Team A is done, the next new-and-improved version becomes Team B's job. While Team B picks up the gauntlet, the original team starts on something completely different. Members of Team A feel satisfied by their accomplishments and can savor the moment while gaining enthusiasm for their next undertaking. Meanwhile, Team B is motivated to top its predecessor with improvements that the first group may not have even envisioned. This method will keep complacency at bay and help you create a culture of innovation where everyone is focused on two things: doing their current job at the highest level, and constantly thinking about what's next. Competition within your own organization sure beats the competition that comes from outside.

You must also give your people the opportunity to explore, to think, and to dream. You won't be perceived as the Wicked Witch (or Warlock) of the West, but instead as the leader with a recipe for winning—one who knows how and when to stir the pot and let it simmer for success.

If you're still not convinced, think of it like this: Previously tried-and-true methods, products, and services may not apply to the future—even if they're working right now—and could be hazardous to your very existence. There is a life cycle for everything, and the clock is always ticking. Just look at products like the rotary phone and buggy whips, washboards and big propeller passenger airplanes. They served a purpose, but their time came and went. This happens all the time; something is hot, and people are buying it. Just look around—there are countless examples of great ideas that were translated into a finished "must-have" product, only to wilt and die on the vine in short order. Do you remember Polaroid instant cameras, Sony Betamax recorders, or Microsoft's WebTV? All were initially heralded as the next best thing, only to fall from grace when the next generation was introduced by a shrewd and heartless competitor.

No area of a business is exempt from change. Everything is subject to scrutiny, and everyone must search for better ways. Organizations must simultaneously start at the bottom and the top and meet in the middle to ensure that they examine every aspect of their go-to-market process and strategy. The goal is to find ways to increase revenue while reducing expenses. Despite the fact that this sounds almost ridiculously simple, a surprising number of companies don't think this way.

Organizations in this new era must cut out fat and simultaneously strive to add initiatives that can produce a satisfactory return on a new investment of money and effort. Inertia is the enemy. Leaders must also ensure that everyone in the organization knows the promise to the customer. Retailing has what is called a *never out list*—items that the store must absolutely have on its shelves for customers at all times. If, for example, you operate a grocery store, you can never be out of milk or bread. If the store starts to run low and these items can't be replenished through normal sources, you must go buy them from a competitor rather than disappoint one customer and risk losing that customer forever.

To get my regular fix of where the action really was in OfficeMax's early days, I visited the first store almost daily. I found the store to be extremely busy on one of these quick stops, and also noted with a significant degree of panic that the store was out of copy paper. I immediately summoned the manager and told him to drive down the street to the nearest wholesale club and buy 10 cases of copy paper. He was astonished and thought that I was kidding until I handed him my American Express card. This was a case of doing whatever it takes and keeping a disappointed customer from becoming a former customer.

After the third Max-Wellness store opened in Naples, Florida, I was doing my usual Inspector Clouseau impression, walking around the store and eavesdropping on customers' actions and comments. On one particular afternoon, I heard two people asking where the pet vitamins were. I immediately picked up my cell phone and called our executive vice president of merchandising to start the ball rolling in finding a source for these products.

I then took out my trusty Olympus recorder and dictated the language that I wanted to appear on the sign over the section for pet vitamins. The copy read: "Pets Need Answers for Healthy Living Too." This mirrored the Max-Wellness theme line—Answers for Healthy Living—that is prominently displayed in all of our advertising and in-store graphics. By connecting the dots, we were able to add another profitable merchandise offering—and more important, give our customers another reason to keep coming back to the store. After all, most people consider their pets to be family members.

You can begin your own similar challenge process by asking your team to examine everything they're doing, and see if there's a better way. A "better way" might mean eliminating redundant and nonproductive measures, or simplifying overly complicated ones—all while finding new hot buttons that will better serve your customers.

And don't be bashful about promoting the innovative "whatevers" you've imagined that will help your customers survive in this new world order. Don't worry about being a fearmonger who promotes concern about the booby traps that lie ahead; just make sure that when you show the negatives, you also serve up solutions. Your customers are always searching for new ideas that benefit them.

Ask your direct reports to make two lists: one including the tasks they currently complete as possible candidates to change, and a second that lists new initiatives that could potentially boost revenue and produce a return. Make sure as well that all of your direct reports have their people perform this same exercise. And most important, make sure that you have a means of "measuring" these ideas. You can't just announce a need for change without creating a formal process to vet each worthy recommendation. If you follow this process, you will have a series of initiatives to help you take the next step in short order. And even if only a few pan out, you'll be ahead of the game.

20

Lesson #20:
Is Perception Reality? How to
Manage Risk, Take Chances,
and Remain Standing

BEING AN ENTREPRENEUR is more about perception than reality. Inexperienced people tend to think that an entrepreneur is much like the gunslinger type who walks into a bar wearing his 10-gallon hat and cowboy boots—and that everyone in the place scatters at the sight of him. There are similar characteristics envisioned about the person who starts a business from scratch. Entrepreneurs can easily gain a reputation as macho gunslingers who didn't do much planning, failed to worry about anything, never took aim before firing—yet always seemed to hit the target. Although this makes for a good silver screen character, a real-life entrepreneur doesn't even come close.

Although I am known as a member of this unique breed, this traditional image doesn't fit me at all. Instead, I have always considered myself a methodical thinker who knew how to take small steps first and minimize reckless risks. In my view, risk-taking is the culmination of assessing the positives and negatives, determining the probabilities, and then acting. This process has taught me how to make smart decisions in minutes, hours, and days instead of rethinking every move ad nauseam. I also don't ever recall deciding anything on a whim, at least not when it came to my businesses, making money, and winning.

I am also very much a numbers- and fact-based CEO, much like the famous line in *Jerry Maguire*, where Jerry's client, pro football wide receiver Rod Tidwell, tells him, "Show me the money!" My self-description fits many other entrepreneurs I have worked with or met. With that as my guiding principle, I have no problem spending serious money to get a good return. However, I have a huge problem spending money without any thought or rationalization about a return.

This doesn't mean that every risk must be 100 percent guaranteed; rather, it's a game of statistics and probabilities. If you do this, then there should be a cause and effect; or, in scientific terms, every action has a reaction. If you're good at what you do, that reaction produces a good profit.

Being able to make mistakes becomes a crucial part of success. Think of it in baseball terms. A star player who bats .333 makes huge money. This gets down to what I'm always telling my people at Max-Wellness as we've gone through the start-up phase: If you are batting 1.000, you're not taking enough chances and are bound to eventually strike out. More important, being able to make those mistakes through a calculated risk-taking process ensures that no matter what happens—even if something turns out to be a bone-headed mistake—it won't kill your business or you.

We certainly had our share of bad ideas during my time as CEO of OfficeMax. One morning, I had what can only be described as an "aha" moment and suddenly decided that if we treated our retail store customers as business clients then they would have more respect for OfficeMax and view our people as advisers. My simple thinking put it in business terms. No one would ever come to an office and position himself or herself across a desk from somebody they were trying to sell without first introducing themselves and shaking hands.

In my moment of brilliance I asked everyone who worked in the store near my Cleveland home—which was my own personal test laboratory—to do the following: When they encountered someone in the aisle (or in the case of the greeter, when someone entered the store), they should extend their hand, introduce themselves, and ask for the order in the form of saying, "What can I get you today?"

The idea seemed good on the surface. Unfortunately, this epiphany fell flat on its face. Although I was well-intentioned, reality says that an 18-year-old kid fighting acne working in the store approaching a customer with an outstretched hand just doesn't fly. Although my bad idea really didn't do much harm, we did have several tense moments when customers couldn't interpret what the kid had in mind and clutched their wallets. I always preach that one must go from mind to market faster than anyone else, so I also believe in cutting one's losses quickly. After a day or two observing the mistake close-up while I lurked in the store's aisles, I bagged my concept as simply a dumb idea.

We learned a valuable lesson: At least in the retail setting, the customer wants a degree of anonymity, and doesn't desire any type of physical contact with employees. More important, they do not want someone in their face. That didn't mean that there could *never* be a handshake. Indeed, this often occurred after an associate spent time with a customer, and the customer was pleased because of the good service and degree of bonding that took place.

I shared the experience with my team at the corporate headquarters, as well as in the stores, as an example to prove I was actually human and did have my share of bad ideas. I also explained that I at least knew when to cut my losses and back-pedal with a degree of alacrity and—I hope—style.

Another such near-disaster came after the anthrax mail attacks of 2001, when I determined that every office worker in the United States would undoubtedly be wearing latex gloves and a facemask in no time. Accordingly, I usurped the vice president of merchandising and had him order a category manager to stock up immediately in every store we had in operation on gloves and masks while supplies lasted.

Like many things hyped in the media from a safety and health perspective, this fear of anthrax never produced a major groundswell or the need for protective clothing. This decision probably cost us some serious money because of subsequent markdowns to erase my bad call. But in the end, we donated the gloves to emergency safety workers and received a healthy dose of good public relations.

There have been other times when I've listened to friends or acquaintances who told me that our stores should carry different types of merchandise. Rarely did those work out. The bottom line is that all CEOs—in the smallest, biggest, and everywhere-in-between enterprises—must know who their customers are and what they want. Sometimes the executive needs that information before a customer even knows. The practice of imposing one's own ideas and personal preferences can lead to failure, unless the idea is applicable to the customer who actually shops in the store and buys the product or service.

Here's an example. The CEOs of companies such as Dollar General or the Dollar Stores, which cater to lower-end customers, can probably afford to buy the highest-end jewelry or Gucci merchandise for themselves or their families. However, those CEOs would never consider carrying this same expensive merchandise in their stores just because they personally liked these products. It is a cardinal rule that must never be broken: Know your customers and understand why they spend money with you. A company can never be all things to all people.

Another important lesson is that selling something just to bring in revenue is like being hooked on crack cocaine. It might feel good for a short period, but it can ruin your life as you become addicted to the sound of ringing the cash register without regard to margins.

In 1996 and 1997 we were losing money on many of the computers that we sold because we were selling them at cost or below. But we wised up and became the first retail chain to bite the bullet and actually get out of the computer business for about a year. As a result, Wall Street hailed our decision, despite its unpopularity with vendors and consumers. Vendors hated our move because we dried up a lot of business we'd been doing with them.

But that wasn't the end of the story. I took a step back and viewed our mistake through a different lens—by asking myself how we could turn a negative into a positive. And so we did. We came up with a new concept and leased the computer department—along with all of its risks—to the then-industry giant, Gateway Computer, which began running a store within a store, or a Gateway Computer department within each OfficeMax.

Although this initially seemed to be a great idea, Gateway's plan ultimately failed because it, too, got hooked on sales rather than profits and suffered the ultimate consequences. OfficeMax suffered no damage because Gateway had agreed to pay us fixed rent, plus a percentage of the sales. Once again, what could have been a major mistake ended up being a no-risk lifeline as we sold the peripherals at a profit while Gateway sold the computers at a loss.

Throughout its history, OfficeMax became a true study of survival of the fittest, with "fittest" meaning having the right people, continually refining the merchandise and marketing concept, making sure that there was money to achieve the objectives, and ensuring that it was enough money to not have a few mistakes sink the ship.

Despite my inherent belief in the importance of risk-taking, it is still important to keep the spending of capital on a short leash. Human nature in business is that nobody thinks things will ever get bad when times are good or great. And when they're bad, very few think they'll ever get better. It's a major danger for any CEO to indiscriminately loosen the purse strings and spend money just because the company has it. In my experience, a company can lose more money in good times than bad. This often occurs because the CEO and the company's top management are sloppy in capital allocations, instead of scrupulously monitoring where every dollar is spent and making sure that there is at least a fairly good chance that the company will receive a return on the investment.

Risk-taking should be a main component of that spending. Make it mandatory that everyone involved knows what the expected return should be on the investment before allocating money to *any* new project. This is known as internal rate of return or IRR. This company has to earn a better return on whatever it undertakes that is both commensurate with the risk and better than just leaving the money in the bank.

When organizations don't do this—and instead just throw money around because it's available—it becomes the first sign of a spreading chink in a company's armor and, often, a precursor to the CEO losing his or her fear of failure. Without a certain degree of fear, a team can become oblivious to the potential of failing.

However, it is just as important to never consider it a mistake when you aspire to achieve perfection and fall just short. People who strive for—and refuse to accept anything less than—perfection often fall in love with the notion of a project or plan with zero defects. This is a terrific idea, but it is totally impractical and typically unobtainable. There is a high cost associated with being perfect; in retail especially, it all gets down to the belief that "in the land of the blind, the one-eyed man or woman is king or queen." This simply means that you need to determine how much better the product needs to be to gain market share and supplant your competition. As far as I'm concerned, one of the few places for zero defects is with the airplane on which I am flying. But in business, it's critical for you as the leader to teach associates that everything is a matter of degree.

Sometimes, if you're driving in a snowstorm, it's enough to simply clean off the windshield, side windows, and rear window of the car. You can see where you're going, and it gets the job done. There's no value to cleaning the roof and the fenders. Leadership and wisdom therefore become the ability to make this kind of determination—what needs to get done versus what is just extra.

21

Lesson #21:
How to Keep Lethargy at Bay . . . Or Why Time Is Your Most Precious Resource

ONE OF THE most treacherous inhibitors of success—as I mentioned previously—is inertia. This is especially true once a new company is up and running. After enduring the exhausting process of getting the doors opened, it's easy for one to succumb and quickly become fat, dumb, and happy. Certainly, after the trauma of making it through the early stages, actually getting a business going should garner a major celebration. The goal, however, is to temper the celebration with the reality that this is merely the first step to success.

Building a business is a series of wins and losses, and the occasional painful setbacks. In fact, during the early stages, a few carefully orchestrated hindrances and minor failures can provide an important wake-up call to the team that reminds them that the company is not invincible. As the leader, you must try to keep your team from taking winning for granted. It is important to have a certain tension within every organization that occasionally keeps team members up at night. This restlessness can be an important catalyst for a 3 AM eureka moment, when you're suddenly awakened with a thought that maybe you should have done this or that, or you worry that the team forgot to consider a critical point. Since this prevents complacency, it can be healthy—because complacency tends to breed lethargy. And lethargy is one of an entrepreneur's biggest foes.

The best method to keep people thinking and progressing is to feed them a continual abundance of information about what competitors and customers are up to. This leads them to contemplate how their own thinking could change. There are countless sources nowadays by way of the Internet to monitor competitors and customer attitudes. A good leader provides a constant flow of new information to the team, sometimes with a pointed question that challenges them to think and then rethink current strategy and next steps.

It all gets down to time, money, and energy; seldom is there enough. The benevolent dictator must be the one who determines how much time should be spent on a given undertaking, as well as how—and how much—money should be allocated. Wasted time and motion become management's Trojan horse, as they seep into your organization and erode progress. If you're not paying attention, before you know it, you've let complacency ooze in. That's when time not spent accomplishing specific objectives will lead the company through treacherous detours.

Leadership must have time to think and act, and avoid distractions (like a money-borrowing, long-lost, deadbeat relative). It's also critical to tackle the most difficult undertaking first and head-on, rather than starting with the easiest. The easy tasks in well-established businesses are also known as busy-work—the kind of things that really won't make a difference at the end of the day.

To do this, you must communicate the facts clearly to all constituents, and emphasize the cold reality of what must be done to continue the company's momentum. Most organizations need less talk and more meaningful actions and results. For example, the average executive nowadays receives more than 100 daily e-mails, and spends more than eight hours a week on electronic communications. We have to establish new definitions as to what "keeping one in the loop" really means. Do leaders really need to know every painful detail of what's happening with all of their direct reports? Descending into this kind of minutiae will take you away from strategizing and making the important decisions. You must reintroduce alternative methods of communication, such as the unique practice of requiring team members to actually *talk* to each other rather than texting one another from a next-door office or cubicle.

Today, more so than ever, time means money—and must be coveted like one of the most precious assets on your balance sheet. If the clock stops ticking and you run out of time, you most likely will run out of money eventually as well.

Empower your key people to make their own decisions to keep moving forward. Teach them to think twice before sending an unnecessary e-mail or placing a phone call by asking themselves, "What is it I want to report? Is it just 'nice to know,' or is it truly necessary information? Will the initial message require another follow-up communication in the next few hours or days?" Train your team members to ensure that the message is complete and includes the who, what, why, where, when, and, sometimes, how of the subject matter before they hit "send."

There is nothing worse than receiving an incomplete message, which then requires an e-mail reply asking for clarification. Make the following rule: If your people send you a message, it must be informative and actionable, not just an FYI that has morphed into a CYA.

Additionally, instruct your team members to set predetermined follow-up dates on everything of importance. If someone knows they're going to miss a deadline, he or she must inform the pertinent parties before the clock strikes 12 on the appointed day. It's not just a matter of common courtesy; it is about saving extraneous effort. As these new standards and processes begin to permeate the organization, you'll find everyone becoming more focused, and much more goal- and task-oriented. Working smarter, not just harder, must become part of your company's DNA.

I, like many people, have spent much of my business career time-stressed and time-pressed. But as I've taught my team to find better ways to use their time over the years, I have also employed a degree of discipline in almost everything I do. I've attempted to combine this with a modicum of creativity to deal with my impatience over wasting time and unacceptable levels of productivity for people and myself. Instead of complaining to anyone and everyone about things that waste my time, I've taken proactive steps to increase my productivity. As an added bonus, I can also ameliorate certain unpleasant experiences ranging from enduring a dentist appointment to sitting through a skull-numbing event.

What's my Holy Grail answer to keep you from lamenting the loss of every second of down time? It starts with a mental agenda. Here is the method I use. Deep in the left side of your brain, create your own "my agenda" folder. Use this to mentally compile a list of things that you must do—such as preparing a report or dealing with an unreceptive employee. If you're not comfortable with this mental storage process, write your agenda on an index card and keep it with you.

Case in point: You're sitting in the dentist's chair as the hygienist fires irrelevant questions at you in between the frequent one-word command of "Rinse." Given the natural apprehension of being at the dentist's office and having someone fussing in your mouth, you immediately launch your cerebral to-do list. Click on the personal mental agenda you previously etched in your memory. Now choose one of the specific items you've stored away, and organize the material in your head. Utilizing both visual imagery and an interior soliloquy, begin preparing your mental work product, much as you would do if at your computer or with pen in hand. Before you know it, the unpleasantness of the event from which you have taken a mental hiatus has concluded.

After the hygienist removes that antiseptic-smelling plastic bib and launches into the obligatory diatribe about advanced flossing techniques, you must move quickly to capture the fruits of your thought-processing session. I recommend carrying index cards or dictating into a digital recorder, as I do. In a pinch, you can always download by writing on the palm of your hand (preferably in nonindelible ink). Sometimes, under dire straits, I have been known to write on my shirt cuff; however, I limit this to only my greatest ideas. After disciplining yourself and overcoming a few false starts, this mental regimen will become a way of life.

This newly acquired productivity tool trains you to translate your thoughts and ideas into actionable realities that can accomplish objectives. It is also a great way to rehearse important messages that you want to preciously deliver. Plus, this technique keeps your mind in gear and progresses your important agenda items.

After six months of using these mental gymnastics, you will have unleashed your creativity and dramatically expanded your capabilities. You'll become more productive, work fewer hours per week sitting behind a desk, and extend your abilities as a true mobile executive. You'll think more and worry less about delays. Eventually, your brain will become hardwired to go immediately from stand-by mode to real-time creating. And you'll make great strides in your own personal battle against inertia. Moreover, you will be entitled to check yes on that time-management box on your personal card.

22

Lesson #22:
How to Avoid Analysis Paralysis by Learning When to Make "Battlefield" Decisions

Keep in mind as you maneuver your way to success that there is a delicate balance between using facts and employing intuition to make important decisions. Combining the use of both the right brain for creativity and the left brain for analytics has been the formula for many great success stories.

Under certain circumstances, it makes sense to drill down on what needs to be done, and then, as I've written repeatedly in this book, for emphasis—"just do it." This method uses the right cranial hemisphere and is recommended for scenarios in which you are well-versed on the subject and have successfully done something similar in either your current role or another life.

More often than not, you need to build a tightly crafted road map. A structure like this will take you through each step in detail—whether the process involves launching a new product or service, starting a company, or reformulating a troublesome strategy. It is not only understanding the variables and paybacks in these cases; it's also a matter of down-and-dirty scrounging for the available information, and then testing and analyzing assumptions and hypotheses before proceeding.

Analysis is a prerequisite to establishing parameters and arriving at a decision. The process must often include a healthy dose of recalculations when applicable to rethink pieces and parts of a project for either a sanity check or just a double check. Before passing the point of no return, you must digest and interpret data based on facts and forecasts to figure out how to proceed with an undertaking. It is pure bravado to pioneer without first learning from what others have done previously to determine what worked and what didn't.

Analysis traditionally is an integral piece of any puzzle. However, analysis can be—and often is—used ad nauseam. In many cases, analysis can lead to that dreaded paralysis, which can be fatal in business.

In a perfect world, one uses both hard-core analysis and creativity as the tools to reach a conclusion. The best executives use their heads (for analysis), their hearts (for supplying the passion and inspiration), and their guts (for intuitively propelling them in the right direction). On a bad day, any one of these faculties will get you through the decision-making gauntlet. On a good day, all three kick in, and suddenly, you can see through those clouds that have plagued your project, leading to the granddaddy of all solutions. In addition, it can happen quickly but you have to watch for the early signs of clearing.

However, there can be a substantial disadvantage to incorporating too much analysis. This occurs when one wants to achieve "zero risk" through even more study and research before pulling the trigger. Analysis then becomes an excuse for either delaying or failing to make a final decision.

Unbeknownst to myself, I began to emerge as a benevolent dictator under fire during the first year of OfficeMax. When we had to move from mind to market and implement must-make changes, I didn't have the luxury of time to build consensus and sway the team to my best guess as to what would work and what wouldn't. Instead, I had to make many announcements that became gospel. It wasn't that my decisions were always better than someone else's; I simply knew that a decision had to be made, and there wasn't time for debate. Even worse, most members of the team were not willing to put their futures on the line and risk that they might be wrong. On the other hand, I knew that I could quickly maneuver around a bad decision if I was wrong—without worrying about political implications.

Sure, I was just as scared as the next guy, and I frequently felt like a schoolyard bully putting my decisions into practice. Everyone wants to be liked and I was no exception. That's when the idea—which came from a movie I had seen years earlier—hit me. The flick was 1970's *Love Story*, starting Ali MacGraw and Ryan O'Neal, where the line "Love means never having to say you're sorry" became ingrained in that era's pop culture. I thought this would be the perfect preface for strong-armed decisions, and accordingly gave my team a quick synopsis of this movie and the background behind the statement as it became part of our early corporate culture.

After this tutorial I occasionally interspersed this line because I knew I'd been aggressive in getting everyone in attendance over to my way of thinking on a particular subject. I found that people would be more likely to accept my actions if I 'fessed up. I let them know that whatever we discussed in meetings would be treated as confidential. In addition, I explained that when I ask for something it should be inferred that I said, "Please." Further, when they gave it to me, it should be implied that I said, "Thank you," despite the fact that I periodically omitted these pleasantries.

Interestingly, I learned people are willing to do just about anything as long as you're honest about your intentions rather than making up some b.s. theory about why you act strangely or aggressively. We were moving so fast in those days that team members either accepted the ground rules or moved on to another endeavor. Most of them stayed and appreciated the directness, primarily because they respected and understood our need to forge ahead and make decisions, imperfect as some seemed. In addition, they were sometimes shocked to see that our ragtag start-up was working—and that what I had predicted would happen really *did*.

I was forced to make so many decisions on the fly that I resigned myself to remain consistent and not fall victim to analysis paralysis. Instead, I learned how to make in-the-trenches decisions quickly, taking whatever information was available and using it to make smart, calculated choices. This allowed me to navigate around the minefields and seize the opportunities that presented themselves without dealing with a lot of bureaucracy.

By April 1, 1989—one year after we embarked on the OfficeMax adventure—I had come to realize several things. First, I had underestimated the amount of personal energy and emotional commitment necessary to start a company with nothing more than a mere idea, a blank piece of paper, and mostly OPM. Second, the job of leading such a company was a 24/7 undertaking. Third, nearly every decision I faced put me in the position of a quarterback on the field; I watched the play develop quickly, and then reacted instinctively, sometimes getting by using my best guess.

The analysis and deeper thinking usually occurred at night for me. Before I went to bed—somewhere between 1 AM and 2 AM—I would think about the biggest challenges that needed solutions and answers for the next day. I had read a lot about subconscious and subliminal thinking, and had determined—in my own unscientific way—that if I could focus on a problem, my subconscious would help me come up with plans A, B, and C. Amazingly, I would frequently wake up after four or five hours of sleep and presto—I would have answers (or at least possible answers) to the problems I had been pondering when I went to bed.

Then, I would hit the ground running every morning. I'd be at my desk by 7:30 AM and ready to tackle whatever came my way. I would use my trusty Olympus recorder and dictate the big ideas I had come up with from the previous night's slumber.

I tried to spend at least a half-hour every morning just thinking rather than doing. One of the biggest mistakes entrepreneurs make during their early start-up phases is to do the opposite—to spend too much time doing and not enough thinking. I have a theory that thinking is unpleasant and painful for most people, and that is causes angst and discomfort between the ears. However, I personally have found the thinking portion of building companies to be the most enjoyable over the years. I truly love playing the "What if?" games in my head. Many of those ideas that I thought were so great when I thought of them— and even after I dictated the outline—turned out to be real dogs, while others were home runs. Either way, my thinking process gave me the opportunity to explore other alternatives.

So here we were, 12 months after day one, and OfficeMax was still in business. We'd actually grown nicely and were operating stores in Ohio, New York, and Michigan. Better yet, we'd done so with no real casualties and just a few wounds. In hindsight, the key to that first year's success was our ability to make on-the-run decisions rather than conduct lengthy analysis that would have meant waiting weeks—if not months—before taking the next step. One drawback was that because I became fanatical about the use of my time, I sometimes failed to take the time to smell the roses and enjoy what we were accomplishing. That has changed today. Much like a fine wine, my experiences have aged gracefully and my memories of the very early days of OfficeMax are a source of great satisfaction and even better war stories.

I also learned during this time that procrastinating or taking half measures to solve problems only made things worse. The winners in business are the people who can move from mind to market faster than the competition. That means making quick-yet-thoughtful choices and taking calculated risks. My own method for making difficult choices was to follow the time-tested formula of ready, aim, fire. I took emotion out of the equation, gathered the facts, decided where I wanted to go, and determined how I planned to get there.

My approach also meant that I couldn't try to please everybody, because that just doesn't happen. I certainly appreciated the effect that my decisions would have on all of our constituents, starting with customers; without them, of course, we wouldn't have a business. I also sought thoughtful input from my associates, employees, investors, and advisers—but not necessarily in that order.

Finally, and most significantly, I learned not to make a decision based on how it would affect "us" or "them." Instead, I made the decision "for the love of the company" and the good of the entity. I learned that by putting the organization before any kind of special interest groups, I would win many more times than I'd lose.

Decisions are not supposed to be easy. Business is not a popularity contest. To make your move, you must listen and learn. Always study the consequences of your decision from all perspectives—short-term, intermediate-term, and long-term. You've got to lead, follow, or get out of the way—make your decision, and then build consensus with anyone and everyone who will listen to you. Speak with passion and conviction, and always have your facts and figures at your fingertips.

Sure, some in the "us" camp will disrespect you, and many of the "thems" will dis you at every turn. Others will refuse to utter your name and refer to you as a pronoun "who shall not be named." But rest easy. You made your decision for the greater good and the love of the company. All things being equal, you will not only survive, but also succeed. Remember that although it's sometimes lonely at the top, the view is truly spectacular.

23

Lesson #23:
Don't Drink Your Own
Bathwater—You Could Choke

As a company approaches a milestone—whether it is opening a new store, launching a new product, or employing a new process—it is important for the CEO to become the CCO: Chief Congratulatory Officer.

Depending on the company's culture, those ceremonial congratulations can take many forms. It might mean an all-out bash with champagne and caviar or giving everybody who has worked around the clock a few days off. A bonus, monetary or otherwise, also works, as does a simple, quiet dinner with time for reflecting on the achievements you've obtained as a group. Different degrees of success will determine how to recognize the accomplishment. What form the celebration takes isn't as important as the actual time to pause and say, "The team is appreciated."

A crucial part of whatever celebration you decide to hold is to encourage team members to rehash both the good and the bad parts of the undertaking. These replays tend to take on a life of their own and improve with age. Certainly, this pause is instructive as those who were involved rethink what worked and what didn't. It's also therapeutic, a healing process of sorts for those whose toes were stepped on or whose noses may have been pushed out of joint in the heat of battle. The celebration gives the team time to savor the moment and imbues in them that intangible and hard-to-describe sense of what it feels like to win.

However, there's one chief danger that awaits every company, entrepreneur, and employee who reaches this point. They are in jeopardy of beginning to drink their own bathwater, which is a crass way of saying that they start believing their own spin and propaganda. History tends to be rewritten about who did what, why, and how victory was snatched from the jaws of defeat.

At a certain level, this is all well and good. The problem arises when the true story gets filtered down and the lessons from the experience lose their meaning because they're not accurate or are too vague. This makes it increasingly difficult to apply what you learned to similar future efforts. If something didn't work and no one remembers why, you're usually destined to repeat past mistakes.

This is why I always require a postmortem that goes into sometimes excruciating details on all significant projects. This is much like we're accustomed to seeing in our favorite cop movies; after a shooting, internal affairs shows up and re-creates the event, then comes to a conclusion as to what really occurred. Although everyone usually hates the internal affairs officers, they serve a purpose: This type of chronicled assessment can greatly help businesspeople better understand how to do what they've done more efficiently the next time.

For example, we realized when establishing the first proto-type Max-Wellness store that it had to have desired visual acuity. This simply meant that the customer could see the back of the store from the front without any obstructions. However, once the fixtures arrived, we knew this would be a problem. The person responsible for sizing the fixtures must have been an NBA ballplayer who assumed that, like him, everyone was over six feet tall. Once it became apparent there was an error, the setup crew decided to cut down the fixtures, which solved the problem. However, I called a time-out. I wanted to document this transgression—not to find someone to punish, but to ensure that we never repeated the same mistake. To this end, we videotaped everything—and also took still photos—so that we had a before-and-after, full-color visual of what the customer should see based on making the fixtures the right height.

Some team members didn't like this documentation process because it would serve as a permanent reminder of what went wrong, particularly at bonus time. However, by handling the problem—and the subsequent remedy—in this way, we had a lesson that no one would forget—one that would surely save us time and money in future stores.

Successful leaders know that the sweet taste of success can be addictive and a powerful motivator for team members to continue to dream, dare, and do. Companies that continue to rack up win after win seem to have a culture that thrives on challenge and repeated success.

The old adage of the customer question "What have you done for us lately?" is a fact of business. Sure, it's great to celebrate, but the team needs to know when to roll up the carpet and end the party. Too many companies rest on their laurels and risk losing their edge while the band continues to play.

So how do you know you're on the right track when the party is over?

It's likely that you'll receive different stories from various people, depending on the colleagues with whom you discuss the particular undertaking. Much relates to how and from what prospective one is interpreting the results. This is why I fine-tuned my philosophy of "trust but verify" long ago. I'm not a cynic, just a realist. People have a need to present everything in the best light. One can make the worst problem seem trivial merely by omitting some of the gory details.

My process—to trust by using my head, heart, and gut—is just the first step. I verify by talking with customers, suppliers, and lower-level employees. It's important to remember that a ringing cash register doesn't always indicate complete verification. Many times a company will introduce products and launch stores with a certain teaser—a giveaway price or a companion offer, as in buy one, get one free, or pay us when you feel like it terms. That means that the customer will buy certain products at the beginning at this too-good-to-be-true price. The question is whether the organization can sustain this momentum, and then accelerate when the price normalizes. This kind of low price sets the bar too often; then, when the price is raised, customers head for the exit sign. It's therefore worth using metrics to determine exactly where you stand.

The Holy Grail of measurement in retail has long been "same store sales"—also known as comparable store sales. This is simply a measure of a store or chain's growth versus the comparable day, week, month, or quarter of the preceding year. You must additionally factor inflation/deflation and external circumstances into this measurement. For example, if a chain has a sales increase of 5 percent, yet inflation is running at 10 percent, the chain is really at a negative 5 percent. In instances with no prior-year results, companies must establish some form of measurement—perhaps the initial plan augmented by monthly or quarterly forecasts.

Looking at these measurements lets organizations quickly analyze success and benchmark whether it's a flash in the pan or something real that can be duplicated.

To determine whether your offering is viable, you need to use many metrics to forecast future sales and profitability. It's perfectly fine to employ a strategy to incur losses on certain products if doing so leads to bringing in more customers and increases volume that leverages fixed costs. Supermarkets invented this tactic to increase traffic, knowing that they wouldn't make a penny on selling a quart of milk, for example. But milk served to motivate the customer to buy something on which the milk could be poured, such as more profitable cereal or fruits. That's why you'll frequently see in good retailers the bargain next to other products that go nicely with the bargain.

Never have illusions that you're the world's best seller just because you happen to be giving it away at the moment. Whether you have hit your stride or have reached a milestone, it's imperative to remember one thing: If you don't remain hungry to achieve continued success, you'll soon find yourself believing that you are as great as your last success. Moreover, if you do that, you could drown drinking your own bathwater or making bad mistakes because you trusted without verifying.

24

Lesson #24:
When the Wolf's at the Door, What You Do Can Make the Difference between Living to Fight Another Day and Going Down for the Count

IF YOU HAVE a business, you're inevitably going to have problems. The trick is learning to deal with the problems and preventing the issues from escalating out of control. You're only fooling yourself when you pretend they don't exist. Therefore, it's how you deal with problems that makes or breaks you and your organization.

In reality, there's nothing wrong with having problems—that is, except when you don't know you're having them. The proverbial streets are littered with executives and entrepreneurs who never knew their operations had problems—either because their employees didn't bring them to their attention or because the bosses didn't tackle the problems and *do* something when they were confronted.

This is exactly why a manager should never shoot the messenger. I had a simple yet effective set of rules that all my direct reports clearly understood as to how they must deliver news to me. First, they had to present any bad news in person—or, when I wasn't available, via telephone. E-mail was strictly forbidden. Although they could communicate good news in any way, the smart ones made it a point to look me in the eyes and deliver their tidings of joy in person. This makes good sense, particularly because it's so important to have quality face time with the boss.

Entrepreneurs and executives who have walled themselves off in an ivory tower tend to operate in a vast vacuum. It's a pretty basic lesson: If no one can get to you, then you're likely to spend your time operating in the dark, and to make habitual false assumptions on the state of the state. This, in turn, leads to bad decisions. Moreover, it isn't much fun to live a sheltered life in a fast-paced company where issues that surface must be addressed rapidly.

Anyone who runs a business—whether a start-up venture or a well-established operation—knows that "stuff" happens when you least expect it. And sometimes that "stuff" can potentially be very damaging. When it is, what should you do when you find that wolf huffing and puffing at your door? How should you, as the CEO, owner, or leader, react to a negative situation?

First, you need to recognize that there are two separate fronts where the issues must be addressed: internally and externally. Both need attention and need to understand how you plan to fix the problem. Usually it's a case when speed counts—and doing the right things at the right time counts even more.

One thing that never works, and that can sometimes dig you into a deeper hole, is to claim immediately and summarily that there is, in fact, *no* problem at all. The worst tactic is to deny, deny, deny before knowing all of the facts, only to find out afterward that there is indeed some real trouble.

Like it or not, perception many times becomes reality. If someone claims there is an issue, then it must become your immediate issue in some form or fashion. The urgency with which you respond to the situation depends on who is doing the huffing and puffing.

Never forget that where there is smoke, there is usually fire. Becoming defensive because you are challenged or because your ego is bruised can set you and your organization up for bigger problems. Reacting with righteous indignation is a no-no.

There are new reports every day about a company that finds itself in the spotlight. Simply read the news and you'll learn of claims being made against myriad organizations—from a public corporation backdating stock options to give the option recipients a lower strike price to facing an environmental claim, safety issues, an accounting problem, or employee harassment charges. Union threats and problems are also guaranteed to send chills down the back of even the most stoic CEO or entrepreneur. Once the accuser—be it a government agency, a shareholder, or an employee—has thrown down the gauntlet, it is time to move to the military's most serious readiness level, DEFCON One, more commonly referred to in the movies as *red alert*.

First and foremost—don't deny anything just yet. Instead, respond by stating that the matter will receive immediate and thorough attention at the highest level of the organization. If appropriate, call on outside specialists to provide a disinterested review.

Never—and I mean *never*—try to sweep a problem of any magnitude under the carpet. After making your initial stopgap announcement, immediately bring your team together and provide leadership by meticulously vetting the initial allegations. Then appoint a spokesperson responsible for responding to all of your constituents, the media, and the public in general. In a time of crisis, an organization must speak with one voice and one voice only. Under certain circumstances and depending on the issue, it may be necessary to remove either a senior person who has a vested interest in the outcome or even yourself from the review process. Impartiality and objectivity are central to resolving the issue quickly and removing any clouds of doubt, suspicion, and emotion.

If you find that the negative assertions are true or even partially true, determine an appropriate course of action commensurate with the problem. You must then take your medicine, no matter how bad it tastes. If that means terminating someone for the transgression, so be it. If it means publicly stating your organization did something wrong, get on with it.

It is mandatory in taking action that you package a comprehensive and forthright response that addresses the issue's cause. Do not insult the public's intelligence by offering up a mere placebo or Band-Aid fix. The public is already cynical about business, so make sure that you do the right thing. It will be easier in the long run. Americans tend to empathize particularly with the downtrodden, provided the company is forthright and lays out what went wrong and how it will be fixed without trying to save face.

If, on the other hand, your due diligence finds that there is no merit to the claim, weigh the cost consideration of the struggle ahead for vindication from an economic, time, effort, and diversion standpoint. As much as I hate to say it, sometimes it's just not worth fighting the fight. However, if there's a chance that your organization will suffer meaningful and measurable damage in any form, then prepare your defense. Have your facts in hand and charge into battle—not in an emotional frenzy but instead by employing a methodical and strategic approach.

It's somewhat like the children's story of "The Three Little Pigs." Just because the wolf said, "Let me in, let me in" doesn't mean all the huffing and puffing will blow your company in. At the end of the story, the wolf got just what he deserved when he was boiled in a kettle of water. Sometimes, there is justice in this world.

There are also precise steps you must take internally to ensure the viability of your enterprise when you hit a bump in the road. Although it is difficult to anticipate every possible crisis, you can develop a general road map that provides a working model to guide you through dealing with problems. You should prepare the plan with the same meticulous thought process that goes into a business or financial plan, a marketing strategy, or dealing with a worst-case scenario.

My own process is rudimentary. When I hit the bump, my first action is to stop, look, and listen. The worst thing that one can do when a big problem arises is to react without complete information. This typically means that someone is treating only the symptoms, not the cause; and many times, a quick superficial fix does more harm than good.

When confronted with a crisis, I usually gather every bit of information that I can. One thing I never do is become emotional or flustered; while I may be crying on the inside, I'm laughing on the outside. A surefire way to derail a company is to let your people know that you're really scared. That leads to panic and magnifies the problem at least twofold. Surveillance and information gathering—by answering the following questions—are paramount.

- How big is the problem, and is there a workaround?
- Is the problem caused by something internal or is it an external force?
- How much time is there to fix it?
- How best to communicate the problem to first your employees, and then your other constituents, such as suppliers, landlords, and so on—and when appropriate, to customers and, depending on the circumstances, the general public?

Once these questions are thoroughly vetted, you can proceed. What initially appears to be a huge problem many times really isn't; just as frequently, a small chink in the armor can cause the entire shield to crumble. The trick is to know the difference.

When you have a good sense that you're dealing with a problem of some magnitude, consider following this series of steps:

1. Determine how you will communicate the issue, and who within the organization you must alert. In crisis mode, there is no time for cover-your-backside e-mail. Instead, spread the word by walking over and telling those who need to know. If those who must be brought into the loop are not all in the same building, try to gather everyone together within a room and/or by telephone conference call. Do it within seconds and minutes, not hours.

2. Have an established method and protocol for gathering as much information as fast as possible on the situation, preferably from someone at ground zero. Designate the people who will manage the problem, and be sure that they have a proven track record of dealing in facts rather than succumbing to emotion. This is no time to have anyone with a

propensity for hyperbole or hysteria on your management response team.

3. If there is a physical or safety problem, take care of people first and assets last. This isn't just good public relations (PR) and associate relations. It is the right thing to do.

4. Rehearse scenarios on how to handle the most likely events. We did it in elementary school with fire drills, and flight attendants do it before a plane takes off.

5. Make sure that the person who is put in charge takes charge. He or she must provide leadership, make decisions, and be prepared to switch to a new plan when appropriate.

When Plan A is not working, have Plan B ready. Don't be afraid to make changes quickly. People need and want to follow during crisis, and there is room for only one leader. Although consensus-building management can be good during business as usual, a benevolent dictator must take over quickly in a predicament.

Let everyone know in advance who is running the show when establishing your crisis plan. Put it in writing instead of letting someone appoint him- or herself as leader when the catastrophe first surfaces.

We all hope, of course, that a dire situation like this never occurs. However, when it does, you must be prepared to triage the situation and have your team ready to take control. There is no genius involved in this process; it is probably 1 percent inspiration and 99 percent perspiration. However, it has worked in the past and it will work in the future when the leader takes charge—and makes sure that everyone else knows it.

Once your business is up and running, it's only a matter of time before the problems begin popping up in unexpected places and at unexpected times. How you deal with the problems will ultimately define your ability to succeed as an entrepreneur. There are always going to be wolves at the door. The big question is whether you let them in or return the favor and do your own huffing and puffing to drive them away—so you can live to fight another day.

25

Lesson #25:
Using the "Mother Rule"
Can Help You Avoid Costly
Hiring Mistakes

FIRING SOMEONE WHO'S not getting it done is unavoidable at times, and should never be easy. People and circumstances change, and sometimes a change solely for the sake of change makes sense. Banishing an alleged wrongdoer to the unemployment line, however, is not a substitute for a bad strategy or ineffective boss. Although it may be an oversimplification, it's easier to hire the right person for the job that needs to get done the first time than to rid the organization of the person who probably shouldn't have been there in the first place.

A bad hire is not only disruptive to the business or organization—it's also expensive. According to a variety of studies, the cost of firing senior- or middle-management personnel can be as high as 300 percent of that person's annual salary, and in some cases even higher. This includes the cost of finding a replacement, training, and the ancillary emotional and unsettling peripheral and disruptive effects.

How can you stack the deck in your favor when making a new hire? Thoroughness, thoroughness, thoroughness. It's shocking how often companies hire an executive without defining the responsibilities, scope of authority, and what the person is expected to accomplish in the short term, intermediate term, and long run. Making a good hire is a methodical process that starts with a need and is followed by a tightly structured job description. Keep redrafting this until you have a fine-tuned outline that provides details on what you expect to accomplish with this addition to your team.

Next, your search begins.

There are numerous ways to find good people. However, when filling top positions, I prefer asking someone who knows somebody who's done it before—and done it well. Once you identify your target, the next stop is to figure out how to make the contact and then pitch the opportunity.

I truly believe that past performance is an accurate barometer of future actions. If someone has been successful in a prior life—and is a hard worker who does what it takes to achieve the goals—then it's probably a good bet that the person will have the same work ethic with you and your organization.

To save time, energy, and travel expenses, I always prefer to start with a get-acquainted telephone interview. Using a webcam enhances the experience by allowing you and the candidate to see each other. If I like what I see and hear, and vice versa, then I schedule a face-to-face meeting. Know as much about this person as you can before the meeting—what he or she has done and, equally important, what he or she has not accomplished. And even if you trust your gut instinct about the candidate, don't fall victim to one of the most deadly sins in business—making snap judgments based on first impressions. You know deep down that you shouldn't judge a book by its cover. Nonetheless, if you feel like you're in a bookstore staring at the dust-covered book jacket of what must be the worst novel on the planet, don't automatically take a pass. Instead, follow these three steps:

1. Salvage the interview and dig deep to find the person's inner strengths and capabilities.
2. If the candidate is from a competitor, gain insight as to why the other guy seems to beat you.
3. Try to figure out a way to make the session professional, doing so in the shortest amount of time acceptable and without the risk of the candidate filing a legal complaint for perceived discrimination. Although rudeness doesn't justify a lawsuit, it can tarnish your own and your company's reputation.

The best course of action is to make intelligent, insightful queries that may penetrate the candidate's negative aesthetic facade. Ask open-ended questions that require the applicant to respond by trying to string together a few intelligent utterances. Never ask yes or no questions; instead, frame your interrogatories in a way that forces candidates to think. Ask them to walk you through a past situation in which they salvaged a bad business situation. Or, have them explain the steps they took to land the best business deal of their career. After 5 or 10 minutes, you may find that the person grows on you and has unique redeeming qualities.

I have found over the years that many of my first impressions have been proven totally inaccurate once I dug a little deeper and determined how someone thinks and communicates under fire and translates concepts into actionable plans. The most success-ful salespeople have learned never to judge a customer who walks into the showroom based solely on garb or physical appearance. The same should apply to your interview process.

Of course, not all interviews or stories have happy endings. About 50 percent of the time, that first gut reaction will probably be closer to the truth. However, you may have the opportunity to discover a diamond in the rough the other 50 percent of the time.

I frequently ask specific questions during the discovery process to which I already know the answers, just to see how the candidate responds. This can be a great way to discern whether a potential employee is giving you pat answers that he or she thinks you want to hear—or is straightforward and honest.

If I had my druthers, I'd speak with a candidate's parents before interviewing him or her. Although this might sound strange, I've learned that some of the keys to success are not necessarily lessons learned in school, but rather those taught at home at an early age. Examples include the fundamentals—integrity, work ethic, and commitment. I also play by the Mother Rule with would-be employees, as well as existing ones: Simply put, if your mother wouldn't approve of what you're doing, don't do it. You'll need to determine the following through the inter-view process when vetting employees: What did their parents instill in them as a baseline for their ethics?

Obviously, it's not possible to interview a candidate's mother and father. However, there are other appropriate ways, which won't get you sued, to delve into an individual's background during the conversation. Much of the procedure is based on how you phrase the questions.

I always ask candidates to think about the opportunity after the interview. I request that they don't tell me on the spot if they're interested. Instead, I ask them to e-mail a letter outlining the level of interest, why they think they can get the job done, and what it would take to entice them to join the organization. This shows me how the candidate thinks and articulates ideas and concepts—and also lets me know if he or she is thorough and intelligent enough to use spell-checker to avoid errors in their letters. Further, it reflects the person's sense of urgency and level of interest based on the length of time until I get a response.

My final step is to have top candidates professionally tested to determine their work styles. There are a variety of accurate and relatively inexpensive work-style assessments that are effective in minimizing your downside and help to ensure that you're not trying to put a square peg in a round hole.

At one time or another, every boss would like to use the now-infamous two simple words "You're fired" to erase the problem of a bad hire. However, when you proclaim the opposite—"You're hired!"—you want to make sure that you've done it the right way for the right reason: your organization's success.

26

Lesson #26:
When Communicating,
Cut to the Chase

Basic communications supposedly started with the cavemen about 130,000 years ago—and those Neanderthals really knew how to cut to the chase and to get their message across. Using symbols and markings, they told what needed to be known: "Where's the food, fire, and danger?" When friend or foe came across the message, they immediately understood.

In 1876, telephone inventor Alexander Graham Bell took a giant communications leap when he spoke through this instrument to a nearby companion device and said, "Mr. Watson, come here. I need you." It was artful in its simplicity (the message, not the phone).

Since those times, there have been huge changes in communications, but as we all know, with innovation comes excess.

Almost everyone nowadays—including businesspeople—often provide TMI in their exchanges: Too Much Information. Rarely do they cut to the chase as succinctly as the cavemen did.

The notion that "time is money" is amplified in today's real-time corporate U.S. environment, when decisions must be made in minutes and hours.

How many of us have had this problem? For instance, we ask a subordinate a basic question, and it takes 15 minutes to get what should have been a 15-second answer. Why do some people have an incessant compulsion to provide minute, detailed responses, embellished with irrelevant "He said, she said" anecdotes?

The answer lies in many people's need to be perceived as an expert. Some subordinates, peers, and even superiors provide this excessive detail in the hope that you will recognize them as the ultimate be-all, end-all authority on the most obscure topics. Ask a simple question—"What time is it?"—and the answer can turn into a rambling monologue on how the watch was built, complete with a sidebar editorial about the precision artisans who built it.

And really—who cares?

Details can certainly provide value in a thorough analysis, but they are superfluous when all you need is a data point or sanity check to proceed in crafting a plan or making a decision. There are a few methods that have worked for me in attempting to get a concise response. The easiest technique is the straightforward approach; however, one size doesn't always fit every exchange. Sometimes you need a lighter, more humorous approach, particularly when you're dealing with sensitive types prone to tears or pouting. The worst-case scenario is when they just don't get the hint—no matter what you say. This may call for the "ton of bricks" methodology as a last resort.

When you use the straightforward approach with someone who is answering your question with voluminous information, you just politely interrupt and state that you recognize him or her as the expert who possesses the intricate knowledge surrounding the subject. Assert that although it's a given that the person knows his or her stuff, you merely need a capsulated 14-second sound bite. With any luck this will quickly lead your associates to give you one- or two-sentence summaries.

Next, assume that someone who's wordy with you is wordy in other situations—including their voice-mail introductions. Survey your employees' current responses for their business e-mail/telephone prerecorded messages and be prepared to be shocked by both the content and the length. Then, to rectify this communication-style shortfall, ask your human resources or public relations staff to put together brief scripts that get the desired message across. Each message should be tailored to the person's job function and provide an alternative contact when there is an immediate need.

Establish standards of what is appropriate. Explain to your employees why you are doing this and that it is another technique to demonstrate how your organization is better than your competition. Callers especially will appreciate the kind of brevity that will allow them to do the talking. Consider ending all voice messages with the same tagline that emphasizes your best attribute, such as "Your satisfaction is our number-one priority" or "Getting to the point makes us better." All Max-Wellness e-mail and voice messages end with our branding tagline, "Be well." This beats gratuitous endings such as "Have a stupendous day."

Most employees will appreciate the scripted assistance, because it gives them one less thing to do. Your clients, customers, vendors, and prospects will prefer it as well; not only will they hear short, to-the-point communication, but they'll also hear a consistent message across your organization. The power of consistency is often underrated but critical to branding.

You'll know that your people are on track when they adopt your techniques to train their own subordinates and associates. They'll pass on the message to simply spit it out and get to the point while sermonizing on the virtues of "time is money." These time-efficiency converts then spawn new time-saver disciples. In short order, you will have created a new legion of one-minute messengers who spend more time thinking and working than they do talking.

Every entrepreneur must learn that communication is a two-way street. Providing clear and concise exchanges is critical. No matter how big or small your organization, you must frequently hold both formal and informal updates with key people. Size should never be a factor that governs the flow of must-know information. Opportunity frequently comes disguised as a negative, and your job is to develop that sixth sense to recognize the issue and then take action.

You must structure lines of reporting and methods of operation to allow you to keep your pulse on the business in real time. Instant communications can work for you—but also against you if the word gets out differently than you wanted.

Some may call you a micromanager for staying on top of the business in this way. I say, "Bunk." If you're in charge, "man up (or woman up)," and then take charge. When things go wrong because someone let something fall through the cracks, nobody is going to remember that you were the Great Delegator. During the first 18 months of OfficeMax, I required every store to call my home seven nights a week to give me sales figures, which I recorded in a ledger. This was easy when we had two or three stores, but it became more of a time commitment when we hit number 25. However, this ritual helped me to manage our growth by knowing our daily cash flow, with an emphasis on accounts payable down to the last few dollars.

Every night before I hit the pillow, I knew what vendors I could pay the next day. Micromanaging? You bet, and proud of it. This protocol not only accelerated our growth but set a management style for executives to operate in a similar know-what's-happening fashion. After our next surge, I reluctantly took my wife's strong suggestion to stop the nocturnal phone calls and graduated to a headquarters answering machine for stores to call.

The devil is in the details. That doesn't mean that the CEO has to manage every single one; however, if he or she doesn't, the top boss must be sure that the person delegated to do so has at least a mild case of paranoia and a smidgen of fear of failure, which keeps the best managers on top of their game. To prevent small, garden-variety problems from accelerating to biblical proportions, you must manage the process and remain aware of the flow of factual information. The delicate balance comes into play in knowing how and when to run the place like a Fortune 500 company, and when to run it like a ma-and-pa store. It all depends on the circumstances.

One size never fits all, and events must dictate your tactics. This means that as the boss, you must instinctively understand when to be an observer and when you must get your hands very dirty, very quickly—in order to survive, succeed, or excel.

You also have to think about the message you want to communicate. How many of your assertions start with a negative followed by a litany of unpleasant consequences? Many leaders think it's more forceful and expedient to say it like it is and simply cut to the chase without thinking about how their message is delivered and received. But this style can prove counterproductive.

It's certainly true that you must tell your team members what they need to know, not just what they want to hear. Sprinkling perfume on a smelly problem doesn't make the fragrance better. It just masks the disaster waiting to happen. But too many leaders fall into bad habits of starting with statements like "If we don't increase sales in the next month, we might have to let go of many of you" or "We either save money on expenses, or we go down the tubes." Although these assertions certainly get the point across, they also set a confrontational tone that insinuates that management is a bunch of knuckleheads who think they are above everyone else. It can also trigger an action–reaction that almost taunts the recipient to do exactly the opposite of what you've asked—or simply ignore the entire message. If any of these things happen, then you're the one with the communication problem.

I've stated in earlier chapters that the key to effective management is to accomplish objectives through others. To do so, managers must successfully communicate the current state of affairs along with what must be accomplished. A good initial step is to treat people as participants and partners in the process and as a part of the solution—not the cause of the problem. If your people aren't responding to your messages, then look in the mirror. Instead of blaming your employees, determine if your directives are providing clarity and the appropriate motivation. Ask yourself how you would want to be told something important. Chances are it wouldn't be to "do XYZ"—or face dire consequences without an explanation. Management often does not give employees enough credit for having the ability to grasp the obvious. You can jump-start acceptance by explaining the issue and the anticipated fix by using a logical, positive tone, and focusing on the good rather than the bad.

However—and there is always a however—if the first communiqué does not elicit the expected action, then put the honey in the cupboard and move to Plan B. If some of your people ignored this first sweet-laced mandate, then home in on those who might need a trip to the woodshed to understand what you really meant. Target your second message to the noncompliant laggards with the old-school, stronger-style message, as in "What part of 'no' didn't you understand?" Unless these tardy adopters are dumber than a stump, the lightbulb between their ears will flash with a little nudge, and they'll likely fall into line.

It's also important to understand that the medium is the message in most cases. This means that the vehicle or venue you select to deliver your directive is just as important as the point itself. Delivering a serious concern about sales would be inappropriate as a part of your presentation at, say, a company awards event. Good news should be presented in an upbeat setting, while subjects that are more serious should be delivered in an environment that conveys the message as strictly business. For instance, send an important message in an e-mail with a grabber subject line that reads "Immediate Attention Required, Confidential Information about Our Company's Future." Alternatively, a statement of consequence could be presented verbally by senior management to a small or even larger group, after which attendees would be handed envelopes bearing their names with a reprint of the points delivered verbally. This adds credibility and significance to the message. Remember, however, that a serious message can still be delivered in a positive tone.

Finally, if all else fails, you can always revert to the no-holds-barred technique of telling it like it is without concern for how your team takes it. It's not a preferred method, but when you've no other options, a ton of bricks will get the job done, too.

27

Lesson #27:
Survival Math—Business Is
Not a Zero-Sum Game

EVERY ENTREPRENEUR MUST teach his or her team "survival math." This includes the basics on how to read and understand an income statement and balance sheets. Many a strategy can be improved after everyone involved understands the financial components of the business. Not everyone has to be an accountant, but anyone who contributes to the bottom line must understand how his or her actions impact profitability. I have found that once employees grasp the mystery of debits and credits, even non-financial types can come up with unique ways to make important improvements in an organization's finances.

The first dose of survival math is to convey a critical truth to employees: In order to compete and gain market share, a company may have to sell certain items and services at or even below cost. But in doing so, you and your team can never forget that the mix of products and services must include components of nearly every sale that make up for the unprofitable sales. This is known in retailing as selling "blind items"—products that customers need, but have little or no clue what they should cost. In office supplies, these were little widgets that people absolutely needed to complete a project using strange-looking "bulldog clips" and uniquely shaped binders that are used for presentations—plus all types of unremarkable, but much needed, plastic file folder accessories. Customers either didn't care what these items cost because the amount wasn't too high, they needed them, or they had no idea whether the price was high or low. There is nothing wrong with picking up an extra margin on lesser-known items; this is what enables a company to offer huge savings on loss leaders, and allows both the customer and the company to come out ahead.

Blind items typically have margins of 50 to 60 percent and even more, which goes a long way toward making up for the traffic-generating special values. A savvy entrepreneur—King Camp Gillette—crystallized this theory. Gillette saw that he could improve on marketing the safety razor and realized that he could sell it at a reduced price—or even at cost—and make up the loss with a hefty profit margin on the blades. His idea was that once the blade became dull it would be discarded and replaced by a new one, using the same holder (the razor). To this day, his widely used practice is called the *razor and blades* business model.

It is much easier to employ this model in a manufacturing and merchandising company with multiple products than to do so with companies that are one-trick ponies with a single product or service. Problems appear once a company's product is commoditized. When that happens, the business could easily begin to swirl around the drain because the entrepreneur has nowhere to turn to sell more profitable add-on products.

During my stint as a venture capitalist, I had a rule that I would never invest in a company that had only one product. I learned this lesson at OfficeMax, when we sold only then-popular Gateway computers. Although Gateway made fine computers, having only one brand didn't give our customers enough of a choice. We did, however, do a decent job of offering hundreds of companion items to computers, which was our version of razors and razor blades.

Auto dealers make relatively little money on the basic car they sell, but by positioning the higher-margin items—such as service contracts and fancy entertainment audio upgrade systems—as a necessity, they can make a few extra bucks while offering car buyers a decent price on the car. This technique applies to just about any type of business or service organization.

Another profit destroyer (in addition to failing to manage margins correctly) that survival math must explain is the cost of not getting it right the first time. The economics of doing something over and over can be devastating, and can quickly cause any profit margins to evaporate. When I was at Jo-Ann Fabrics, its custom-made, in-home shopping drapery division reported to me for a few years. Although I was not an expert, I spent the first weeks on the shop floor watching how things were measured and constructed. Then I went to customers' homes to observe the installation.

I was shocked at the imprecise measurements that went into making drapes. I was even more appalled that any incorrectly installed drapes required the installer to come back, take the drapes down, bring them back to the workroom, fix them, and then return to the customer's home to reinstall them. It was clear after enduring that cycle just once that making this a more profitable operation would require significant changes.

I knew nothing about manufacturing at the time, and even less about the drape-measuring business. But I did have common sense—which is what we needed to remedy the problem. I knew that I had to ensure that measurements were correct and that there was a degree of quality in the finished product that matched what the customer ordered. To that end, I held installers accountable through an incentive system. It dictated that any second (or third) visit an installer made to a customer due to his or her error would come out of the installer's pocket. Much like the California penal system, I also employed a strict "three strikes and you're out" program.

When I initially changed the procedure, the longtime employees in the workroom and the installers were ready to revolt. They had been trained for years to "do it quickly." However, the installers and measurers began to apply precision to their process, as well as a series of checkoffs to ensure that they were doing it correctly the first time.

To offset the penalties of making the employees economically responsible for their errors, we also installed a program in which we rewarded the same employees for catching a mistake and fixing it before the damage or the product was manufactured. This got the employees to think about the issue from a perspective where they felt it the most—in their pocketbooks. It was also a classic example of the carrot-and-stick motivator.

The profitability of this little operation improved significantly in a year—so much so that many of my colleagues thought I was a manufacturing wizard. In reality, I had done nothing more than what Henry Ford tried to do: having specialists for each process in an assembly line, rather than making a single person complete every task halfway.

These same lessons apply to any company. Too many organizations focus on increasing sales without bothering to notice whether the customer is satisfied, or if the product or service was produced efficiently and effectively to maximize profitability. It all gets down to "doing it once and doing it right."

Another survival math lesson I learned from my days at OfficeMax is that winning cannot be one-sided. If you constantly win at someone else's expense, then ultimately you—the entrepreneur—lose. In order to engage a supplier, employee, or any other kind of associate, you need to tell them what's in it for them. The good news is that most reasonable people with adequate resources are willing to bet on the "if come" scenario, provided that first, the pitch is plausible; second, the person making the pitch is enthusiastic and sincere; and third, the proposal has a decent chance of succeeding.

Everyone wants to be an entrepreneur deep down inside, or at least wants to be perceived as one. However, few have the stomach, not to mention the know-how, to be one. But if you help teach your team the basics of business math, you'll create a legion of followers who get it and can eventually understand the mathematical sequence for success and the give-and-take needed to make everyone's bottom line work for them.

And the bottom line is that business is not a zero-sum game where another person has to lose in order for you to win.

28

Lesson #28:
Manage by the Three Ps—
Persistence, Perspiration,
and Performance

As a CEO I am fond of saying, "We pay for performance, not perspiration." I use this curt comment when associates constantly remind me—in sometimes not-so-subtle ways—of how hard they are working.

We all know the type. They're the first ones in the office in the morning but, more times than not, they're also the ones spending extra minutes or hours reading the paper, checking the Internet, or calling their long-lost friends and relatives. These managers have an insatiable need for self-promotion and the bragging rights that come with always being the last one standing, or striving to garner the impression of the hardest-working corporate person. They usually become legends . . . in their own minds, at least.

I respect hard work and know that sometimes one has to just gut it through to get the job done—and that takes long hours. There is a definite correlation between success and persistence, perspiration, and performance. Some of the most successful and productive executives I know are also among the hardest workers. The difference, however, between these people and those who talk about how hard they work is that the doers work smart and can demonstrate the fruits of their perspiration. I'll always bet on the manager who knows when it's time to pull an all-nighter to accomplish the big objective and then take a long weekend to recharge his or her batteries over those who just put in the face time—but never seem to reach the goal.

As the size of your team grows along with your company, managing by using the Three-P Formula can help you kick-start your operation into high gear and weed out people who won't help your company reach the next level. It is difficult to strive for success without employing these "Ps." Very few can hit peak performance without a bit of perspiration, and even fewer can get the job done without persistence. Basically, it is hard—and equally rare—for some to perform consistently when relying on only one of these attributes. A good manager knows when to hit each of the three individually, or do so simultaneously.

One way to get started is to develop a system for time and action. I use some methods that are as old as the hills, although now my system is computerized and today has a lot fancier bells and whistles. But whether high-tech or written on the back of an envelope, this system follows a simple timeline that specifies what has to get done by when and by whom. It starts with the person responsible, describes the task, states the appropriate intermediate follow-up steps, and finally identifies an end date. I have used this type of time-and-action plan in just about everything I have done in my career. At Max-Wellness we use a thorough computerized system that is constantly updated as circumstances change.

Building a business from scratch requires an orchestralike conductor, as in the CEO who has the wand. But it is not a magic wand. Rather, it's one used to signal or point to members of the orchestra and invoke a specific action. Many companies fail because, simply put, nobody is calling the shots.

Experience has shown me that when the CEO, owner, or leadership team finally sets definitive goals—be they economic, time-based, or whatever—the good players step in and make it happen. I've also learned that during these high-intensity periods the best of the best have the most fun. They thoroughly enjoy the process and the adrenaline rush it gives them.

No one can run at 100 percent power all of the time, but intervals of elevated intensity and high speed are part of what's needed to accomplish significant objectives. Ask any athlete about training, and he or she will explain the problem of muscle memory. This happens when one continues to do the same exercise at the same pace day after day—there is a diminishing benefit and return. Intervals of speed, on the other hand, surprise muscles and prompt them to react favorably by strengthening. The same theory can be applied to a company. Although one can't burn the candles at both ends forever, the occasional all-nighter does build character and produce results.

My personal work style at OfficeMax was to get to the office early, have a plan for the day, then tackle the most difficult or unpleasant tasks first. It's a great system because the day gets easier hour by hour. And I always left a little time for "management by walking about." It was my way of taking a quick break while assessing the organization by engaging in short conversations with staff members, from clerks to vice presidents. It also let employees know that I was paying attention, that I was accessible, and, most important, that I cared.

Once I completed my rounds, I'd get back at it until I was finished. After ticking off everything from my must-do, to-do list, I moved on to thinking time, meeting with colleagues, or sometimes just schmoozing, bonding, or focusing on new and better ways to get things done.

I would always persevere on what I set out to do, and every once in a while, I'd even note a few dignified beads of perspiration—either figuratively or literally—forming on my forehead as the day progressed. I made a point of making it known to my direct reports team how I approached my day with what I had to get done. As my day ended, usually about 7:30 PM, I'd pack up my briefcase with the hope that my Three-P Formula enabled me to leave the place a little better than it was when I had arrived in the morning.

One of the most fulfilling aspects of using the Three-P Formula is to teach your team discipline and reward. The teaching part encompasses making sure that whoever has to do whatever at least has a starting point and knows the task at hand. A good teacher doesn't necessarily have to know how to do it; however, he or she should be able to explain to the doer how to keep score, how to know when it's not working, and most important, how to know when enough is enough. The answers are somewhere and the teacher has to point the student in the right direction to find them.

It all comes down to discipline, which is an underrated aspect of success. Most people think it's the big idea that works when, in fact, it's the everyday grunt work that gets the big idea to the marketplace. Discipline shows up in a variety of ways, including in someone who has the fortitude to deliver on time as promised. Discipline means not giving up; it means constantly experimenting. It can be someone who does something well and then goes on to figure out how to do it even better. Discipline can also be— figuratively speaking—hitting someone upside the head to get his or her attention. This type of discipline usually occurs when the person lacks the aforementioned characteristics.

My team members know that once all is said and done, they must subscribe to the theory that the journey is as much fun as the destination. That is the essence of what you, as the entrepreneur, must accomplish during Phase Three of your organization's life cycle. You'll promptly discover that when you manage by the Three-P Formula there is certainly a lot of truth in the saying, "The harder you work, the luckier you get." However, just like the deodorant television commercial proclaims: "Never let them see you sweat."

29

Lesson #29:
You Can't Live with
'Em—How to Manage Prima
Donnas, Employees Who
Think "It's Not Their Job,"
and the Perfectionists

YOU'LL QUICKLY LEARN in the early stages of any start-up venture that there are numerous types of employees that you'll have to manage, each a bit differently. Poor performers or high-maintenance employees with an inflated sense of self-importance require a simple solution: Take a page from Donald Trump's playbook and utter those infamous words, "You're fired."

However, the dilemma occurs when you have high-maintenance prima donnas who believe they walk on water and who really are terrific and get the job done (and then some). What's even worse is that they believe they're irreplaceable, and so does everybody else—including you.

You really have only two choices during those early stages: You can rid your organization of this exhausting albatross. Or, you can take the more profitable route, and find a way for a peaceful coexistence by learning how to deal with the performer's short-comings while taking advantage of his or her strengths.

Prima donnas are typically okay people deep down inside. But something went awry somewhere along the way. Either their egos were stroked disproportionally to what they achieved or they suffer from such a severe inferiority complex that they are compelled to tell anyone they can—at every opportunity—how fantastic they are. Although this might sound a bit like the description of a borderline psycho, there's a difference between a prima donna and a psycho: The prima donna gets results.

The trick to managing high-maintenance superstars is to uncover what makes them tick and figure how to push the right buttons to keep them on the straight and narrow while getting maximum output from them. What deeply seated limitation deflates their egos to a manageable level while maintaining their confidence? Is it their need to be the center of attention, or do they thrive on causing chaos, always claiming to be right and starting arguments just to test or fine-tune their debating skills at your expense? Could they sincerely think that they are the best thing since sliced bread? Once you ascertain what pushes their buttons, you are more than halfway to your goal of discovering the silver bullet to neutralize their annoyance factor—but pre-serve their productivity.

Case in point: Your number-two guy is, in fact, a rainmaker who can woo customers and charm their socks off while solving problems with little or no direction. The downside, however, is that everything is a cause célèbre with him. He causes you sleepless nights, disturbs day-to-day operations, and adversely affects morale and productivity.

The easiest solution here is to put your cards on the table. Tell him that he is great, you love him for his good work, but he is a real pain to deal with. Let him know that not only has he reached the point of being tedious, but he is also approaching the cross-roads leading to a place neither of you wants to go.

Ask him what you can do to avoid future problems that are unproductive and distracting to the mission. Also reinforce with him that your door is always open, and he is always welcome to come in, sit down, and vent when he has something to say to you. Make him a part of the solution by putting the onus on him to come up with a fix for a peaceful and productive coexistence. Allow him to win, but on your terms, not his.

Let's say, for example, that this individual wants to announce the big idea he has been working on with you to the entire organization. His main motivation is to prove, once again, that he is the best. Instead of presenting the big plan yourself, let the star performer take center stage. You introduce the concept, but let him tell the story of the idea's incubation to its fruition. A word of caution: You must control this egomaniac's presentation by having a rehearsal to avoid alienating others with uncensored comments.

This is really not much different than how one might manage, say, a six-year-old. You would likely give the child two alternatives from which to choose. The right answer is obvious, but you let the runny-nosed kid decide which fork in the road to take. All of a sudden, the child is taking ownership of the solution, even though you managed him to the right answer without giving up ground.

Prima donnas take more time and attention, but the alternative is losing a high performer—potentially forsaking productivity and inciting some major anxiety. Don't ever forget that prima donnas who produce are a recognized commodity. For good or bad, they are the devil you know.

There's another type of employee who can get under your skin: the person who performs but says, "It's not my job" when asked to expand his or her role. I have a rule at Max-Wellness, and every employee on my team knows it: Their title is "whatever it takes." A successful business must always be a team effort, and at times people need to cross lines to help out. It's as simple as that.

Go to your favorite restaurant and watch the waiter bring a full tray of many entrées to a table. In the best restaurants, seemingly out of nowhere, someone else—a second waiter, a busboy, a manager, or a hostess—appears and starts helping the waiter get the plates to the right patrons. The same teamwork applies in virtually every successful business.

I have come close to firing employees on the spot for repeatedly making the statement "It's not my job" or "It's not my responsibility." Along these same lines, I typically will not hire someone who came from a failed company if they answer the following question incorrectly: What part did you play in the failed company's demise?

I don't care whether the person was a secretary or the former CEO. Business is always a team effort in success just as much as in failure. The appropriate answer is something akin to "I learned an important lesson," followed by an explanation of what they realize in hindsight they could have done differently to have helped the company avoid its problems. I also want to know that they realized that isn't the way to do things correctly in a company. If they approach my question from that perspective, I'd consider inviting them to join the team (as long as they passed all of my other standards).

Another type of problematic employee is the one who strives for perfection and can't accept anything less, even when perfection isn't what's needed for the objective. As we've previously discussed, this can be one of the biggest pitfalls in an early-stage start-up venture. Too many entrepreneurs fail because they try to do something perfectly when the reward for being perfect is not commensurate with the amount of effort it would take to reach that level. When an employee subscribes to that philosophy, the executive in charge must learn to proceed with caution when explaining what must be accomplished and let the associate know how much time is worth putting into the task.

I'm not proposing that you do a lackluster job and not strive to get it right the first time. It also costs the company if someone has to consistently repeat a task to make it work. However, if you're putting out a fire in a garbage can, you can probably get the job done with a few gallons of water rather than bringing in a huge water tanker.

There are always those things that must be done near perfection in major undertakings. There are also numerous tasks that can be just adequate enough to get to the next step or support another initiative.

It can be difficult for people in the fray to distinguish between the two. It is therefore up to you to point out the difference and coach your team members on how to identify it for themselves in the future.

The reality is that most big problems become that way because of a series of little issues that no one paid attention to or cared about. A hem unravels one stitch at a time, and so does a business.

Always keep in mind that you're not marrying a prima donna or any of these difficult personality types. You just need to be able to occasionally dance with them.

30

Lesson #30:
The Golden Rule of Trust and Respect: You've Got to Give to Get

EARNING YOUR EMPLOYEES' trust and respect is neither easy nor automatic; it doesn't happen just because you're the boss or a benevolent dictator. It requires true effort, it must be genuine, and most important, it must be based on your actions—not just your words.

One way to engender trust is to encourage your employees to talk behind your back. Although that may sound like you're proactively fostering the beginnings of a coup d'état, behind-the-back venting can be both constructive and therapeutic if framed correctly.

There are some simple and effective methods to encouraging "employee back-talk time." I discovered when I was CEO of

OfficeMax that I could control this process by structuring a protocol by which all my direct reports could have an open forum to take their best shots at me. I created early on something I called an *operating committee*. This was composed of my direct reports and other key corporate managers and executives who had to carry out company mandates and run the place day in and day out.

I attended only one operating committee meeting, during which I made a statement that took less than a minute. I simply said that this would be my first and last appearance at "your" weekly meetings, and that the group would set its own agenda going forward. I emphasized, however, that there should be back-talk time on every agenda during which participants could vent their frustrations and talk about any heretofore typically unspeakable subject—even if they reflected negatively on my leadership, decisions, or capabilities.

I also let them know that the only thing I asked was that if the committee decided as a group that I was making big mistakes, someone must be appointed to come and tell me—with my promise of immunity from prosecution. I made it clear to the operating committee members that their job was to make me better, and that in order to facilitate that, they could talk about my (real or perceived) shortcomings behind my back or confront me privately.

Now, I didn't just fall off a turnip truck. I knew that not all of the comments would be complimentary. I approached the process in a Machiavellian manner, knowing that if I could get past the bruised ego I could become a more effective CEO and ultimately deliver better results.

Each week my people could identify my errors, which periodically were more than valid. At times, I observed the folks leaving the operating committee meetings with satisfied smirks on their faces. Why? Because they had gotten whatever was bugging them off their chests. They were able to compare notes, and I think realized fairly often that what might have been festering as a "big problem" was not particularly significant in the overall scheme of things.

Another ancillary benefit of this behind-the-back talking is that it tends to defuse situations that might otherwise grow out of proportion. This release technique enables the team to move on to more important matters.

There are a number of other practical ways to foster venting in your organization. It might be appropriate during particularly tense times to excuse yourself from a planned dinner after a day of meetings with employees because your gut tells you that they need to have time to themselves. It takes a certain confidence and a healthy ego for a leader to foster this process. Most of the instances in which I bowed out of a dinner with subordinates, I knew that my employees' ensuing collective catharsis would give them satisfaction and refocus their efforts.

As a leader, you can use similar back-talk techniques to maintain equilibrium in your company and reduce both petty and deep-seated distractions that impede progress. Being a good manager means accomplishing objectives through others. A key element of being a great leader means keeping the team focused and communicating with you and each other.

Another vital way to ensure trust among the troops is to keep your word. Think about the number of times someone has said to you, "I promise I'll get back to you," or "Let's get together and take it to the next step." Now think about what percentage of the time a person uttering these promises actually followed up and made the effort to close the loop. It's probably not very high.

The truth is that most people don't do what they say they are going to do. They're not bad people, and they're not always lazy.

The reasons people don't do what they make commitments to do are varied and numerous. But whatever the reason, these promise breakers miss huge opportunities to take an idea or concept and make something of it. They give up the chance to take advantage of a new business relationship that could lead to something meaningful, where they could actually even make a buck. In addition, they miss the opportunity to build and foster trust with employees.

I quickly learned when I went into business that associates, employees, and even suppliers and contractors frequently just didn't do what they said they'd do. They'd forget to provide the data requested, neglect to come back with a resolution, or just entirely ignore the opportunity or problem. Instead of getting mad, I made it a learning experience that would not be quickly forgotten.

Early in my career, I developed follow-up tactics that were almost foolproof, such as writing myself a note and assigning a follow-up due date the minute I walked out of a meeting or left the person with whom I was talking. This became a compulsion for me, but this simple technique never failed me.

Next, as soon as I was in safe territory, I would write a much more detailed outline of what had transpired—or most times, dictate it on my ubiquitous trusty companion, the Olympus recorder. When transcribed, I'd then put the note in a tickler file. On the appointed date for follow-up, I simply launched my message. I got a response almost every time—and those responses often paved the way for a new deal or a stronger business relationship.

As I moved up the rungs of the management ladder and became the CEO of a Fortune 500 company, I used this tactic after every meeting and encounter, recording for posterity and follow-up what was to happen and by what date. I developed a reputation for having an ironclad memory, a person who never forgot a detail. But as far as I was concerned, I simply wanted to get it done then and there—and then get the task off my plate.

Some people feared me because of my obsession for follow-up and details; and more than a few undoubtedly disliked my style because they couldn't blow one by me. I always held them accountable. The good news is that many more people learned from me. Better yet, I was able to build trust with my team by keeping my word and not breaking my promises.

Earning trust is one thing; earning respect is another. The two, although closely related, are not mutually exclusive.

Most executives usually try to do the right thing. They carry out their responsibilities, weighing the pros and cons of their actions and decisions. However, way too many of them assume that their people will somehow recognize the angst they endure before gaveling an action into effect.

But your employees cannot simply through osmosis understand why you do something—and this is where communication comes into play. How many times have you made an important decision and just filtered it down with what I call the *so be it* method? Sure, sometimes mandates are a part of being a leader; some are popular, and others aren't.

I've learned a number of lessons about respect throughout my career. The most important of these is that respect can be earned in many ways, and most times, it's simply a reflection of your attitude and actions, rather than what you actually say.

When I was a young CEO at OfficeMax, I participated in what are known as Wall Street security analyst field trips, in which an underwriter organizes an excursion that takes portfolio investment professionals on the road with CEOs of similar businesses. One such trip was a bus tour of retail stores in Providence, Rhode Island, visiting each respective CEO's store along the way. The tour included a 45-minute walk-through, during which the chain's CEO explained why his or her operation was the best on the planet.

On this particular tour, everything was running late and my store was the last stop. As the bus arrived, my watch told me there was a huge time problem because participants had planes to catch.

We entered the store to find it spotless; you could literally eat off the floor. All of the employees were wearing their Sunday best. The leader of the tour whispered in my ear that I had 10 minutes to get the message out. As I rushed 20 portfolio managers through the store, talking faster than the pitchman on the classic FedEx commercial years ago, the dejected looks on the employees' faces were apparent. My tour ended almost faster than it began as I walked backward out of the store continuing my pitch.

As we boarded the bus to the airport, I felt lousy. I knew the employees most likely had suffered acute gastrointestinal distress while preparing their store for showtime. As the bus barreled down the freeway, I realized this was a defining moment for me. I called the store manager and told him to get in his car, catch up to my bus, and quickly get me back to the store. Instinctively I knew that I had to show this store's employees that I respected them and their work.

When I returned to the store, the employees gawked at me with eyes bigger than saucers. I then spent about two hours walking the store, aisle by aisle, with all of the employees in tow, asking for their input on everything they did. I missed my plane, had to stay overnight, and ruined my schedule—but it was worth it.

Word of this encore visit spread through our 1,000 stores faster than Grant took Richmond. In no time, this infamous visit turned into a celebrated success and became a part of the company's history.

You, too, can pick your own time and place to re-create a "respect event" that will speak volumes about how you do business. You can do so by arriving at meetings on time and ending the meetings as scheduled. It can also be reflected by not piling on the work just because you decide you need something on your timetable without consideration of what else is currently on someone else's plate.

Respect is contagious; it can incite a cascading trickle-down effect. Your direct reports will begin to increase their respect for subordinates—and even you, if you're lucky. It's not only the right thing to do; it is the correct way to build a business and create a positive culture.

Trust and respect are two of the most critical things you need to have from your team in order to be successful in business. When all else fails, keep in mind that you can improve your business persona by following this golden rule: To get trust and respect, you first have to give them.

31

Lesson #31:
Why You Must Look
at Business through
the Customer's Eyes,
Not Just from an
Operator's Perspective

EVERY GOOD COMPANY today must be an advocate for its customers. The problem, unfortunately, is that most entrepreneurs, presidents, CEOs, and owners often lose sight of this and forget about their reasons for being. They talk a great game and claim to be committed to customer service, but they often either fall short of the mark or fail to follow through on the basics.

In 1976 a satirical movie titled *Network* won four Academy Awards and quickly gained a cultlike following. The flick centers on an anchor newscaster who is fed up with his job and the world around him. His frustration erupts during a live national TV broadcast that galvanizes the nation with the rant, "I'm mad as hell, and I'm not going to take this anymore." This protagonist's action prompts Americans across the country to literally open their windows and shout this defiant pronouncement for any and all to hear.

But that was then, and this is now. And nowadays, it's not a fictional character who has adopted this mantra—but the public at large. Customers now have the power—and they know it. No longer do they have to accept inferior products and dismal service. Most frustrating, according to many surveys, is the plain bad attitude that accompanies many companies' lack of follow-through and poor service.

In our Internet-based world of almost-instant computer-driven communications, blogs, chat rooms, tweets, Facebook pages, and apps galore, the consumer has come of age. There is a fast-growing movement afoot, and customers of the twenty-first century will not be denied.

What does it cost your business when you consistently break promises and disappoint? Most likely, it's not only your potential growth but possibly your existence. Each day that your company turns on the lights and opens the front door, you need to be prepared to keep your promises. Consumers have lost their patience with apathy, incompetence, and rudeness. In these difficult times, a number of companies that have been around for years won't make the next cut. There are simply too many alternatives available for customers to tolerate an inordinate amount of corporate mumbo-jumbo and sleight-of-hand shoddy treatment.

Do employees wake up in the morning and want to do a bad job? Absolutely not. The problem doesn't stem from the employee providing the bad service, but rather from the employers who accept mediocrity and incompetence. In effect, companies become enablers by doing a poor job of training associates and failing to enforce service standards. At the core of the problem are those who don't measure up and who fail to look at issues and opportunities through their customers' eyes. They stand fast to the misguided belief that their perspective as the operator means they know what's best for their customers and think they understand what their customers expect.

But they're wrong on both counts.

To meet or exceed expectations, a company does not have to do anything extraordinary. Most times, just being civil and moderately efficient will win over the vast majority of customers. Yet for a variety of reasons—including expense control and the all-too-prevalent personnel cutbacks—many organizations let customer service go to seed. This thinking flies in the face of good judgment. There is nothing more important than devoting money, time, and resources to the area in which you'll get the best return. Customer service should be the last cut you make before you're forced to permanently turn off the lights.

The daily objective for every owner and corporate executive must be to make their customers' lives a little better and at least more tenable, if not easier. Anything less than this will cause companies to risk becoming targets of newly empowered and technology-savvy customers who know how to spread the word electronically with a cry that could be heard from every open window around the world.

The new reality is that your business stands at a crossroads every time a customer or client is unhappy with your goods or services. Either that customer will become permanently disenchanted or you can seize a short-lived opportunity to strengthen the relationship by turning a negative into a positive.

There is no simple way to guarantee customer satisfaction. However, a good first step is to make sure that you embed the company's sacrosanct policy that customers are always right—even when they're partially or almost entirely wrong—in the hearts and minds of every employee. And this doesn't become a way of doing business simply because it's written in a manual. Management must educate employees about the domino effect caused by unhappy customers who will repeat the company's transgression conceivably anytime there's a lull in conversation. Make sure that your employees also understand the power they possess in their role of problem-solvers to satisfy the customer's problem then and there, with no ifs, ands, or buts.

Once you or your employee reverse a negative experience, the satisfied customer frequently tells others about the positive encounter and the company's fairness. My experience is that the customer who brings up an issue not only wants to right a wrong but is also, many times, subconsciously looking for a reason to continue to do business with the organization. Just as negative comments from the disenchanted can ruin your business, this new believer can help you prosper.

When I was CEO of OfficeMax, we had an army of telephone customer service representatives who were trained to do the right thing for the customer the first time around. The best reps were those who had previously been on the losing end of a negative experience as a customer elsewhere, finding themselves trivialized and demeaned by a would-be problem-solver who only knew how to say no. Periodically, tenacious customers who were outraged by a perceived transgression made it their mission to find a way to reach me directly. The more creative ones would get my private number from an accommodating company operator.

I would identify myself when I personally answered my phone in the evening, and the irate caller would, many times, launch into histrionics. He or she would often suggest that I take the product causing their angst and place it where it shouldn't go and wouldn't fit.

After the ranting and raving stopped, I almost always solved the problem by immediately saying, "I'm very sorry. I apologize. You're right."

Over time I became more creative in dealing with customers who called after-hours. Instead of answering with my name, I would simply say hello and state that I was the computer tech working on the big boss's computer. I would state that all of us at the company were "trained to stop whatever we were doing and help our customers." The caller would then rationally explain his or her problem. Playing the role of the customer-centric tech, I would say that I was writing a note to the CEO explaining the problem and taping it to his computer screen. I also confidently proclaimed that I was sure there would be a resolution by sundown the next business day.

Many times, the customer would ask my name. I would give them a pseudonym and a department number, which, if they called again, would be directed to my office, where my assistants were well aware of my little charades. I received many letters of recognition over the years for that "tech" who took the time to listen and bring the dilemma to the CEO's attention.

We are only as good as our reputations. In my role as the stand-in customer service rep/nighttime computer tech, I knew as soon as I hung up the phone that we would again turn a likely defeat into a resounding victory. These experiences led us to establish a number of nonnegotiables at OfficeMax when it came to the customers who contacted us with complaints. First, a customer had to receive a response within 24 hours. If it was not going to be in their favor, a manager had to approve the response. When we were wrong, the employee had to say the words "I'm sorry." Finally, the issue was promptly documented if it was a valuable lesson. We wanted to ensure that once we had fixed the problem we wouldn't make the same mistake twice. It's a costly problem to duplicate your mistakes and never learn from them.

Whatever kind of business you're running—whether it's a retailer, software development firm, restaurant, accounting firm, or manufacturer—it's imperative to listen to what your customers are really saying when they tell you what they want from your business. You must learn how to think like your customers and see things through their eyes, not just yours. In essence, you must create an environment, a product offering, and a way of doing business that make you the company of choice.

Many business executives have made the fatal mistake of falsely thinking that they could outsmart the customer. Worse yet, they believe that their customer was really only a means to an end—instead of the reason the company existed. When you begin to look at your company from your customers' perspective you'll find that you're much more likely to be able to give customers what they want, when they want it, and at a price they want to pay. Most important of all—you'll find that you actually enjoy doing it.

32

Lesson #32:
When It's Time to Pull
the Trigger and Fire a
Customer or a Vendor

HOW MANY OF us can say we will do business only with people and companies we like and trust? Probably not too many.

Countless employees indulge in the fantasy of telling the boss to take the job and shove it. Meanwhile, the boss's recurring dream is to tell that recalcitrant customer to take his or her business and cram it.

The reality is that not many organizations can afford to do business with only like-minded customers whom they really respect and enjoy. It's a big world out there, and customers come in many shapes and sizes with their own idiosyncrasies and personas—some of which are more tolerable than others. If doing business were limited only to customers whom we liked, there would be no mega law and giant accounting firms. Huge multinational investment banks wouldn't exist, and most corporations would have headquarters in offices the size of phone booths instead of skyscrapers. A nice benefit would be that all of these service firms would save money on rent, but generating enough volume to keep the doors open could be an issue.

The good news is that—just like dealing with your employee prima donnas—you're not marrying your customer either. Much like holding your breath underwater when you were a kid, you can do it regularly for a certain period and be no worse for wear. The more salient question is: Can—and will—you do business with people whom you do not trust or who don't meet your ethical standards?

Every organization must have parameters and an internal gauge that ranks the "like" and "trust" factors. When the internal gauge reaches the proverbial red zone, you must sound the alarm and ask tough questions. At the top of the list is what I call the front-page question: Would your company do something if it had the potential to be reported as a negative lead story in tomorrow's *Wall Street Journal?*

Just as individuals need to develop a moral compass, organizations must employ a similar set of benchmarks or lines in the sand, which, when crossed, put the status of doing future business with any customer in question. Most of us have our price, but compromising our ethics not only is wrong; it can be too costly—despite how important a customer's business might be to the bottom line. If a client's methods wake you up in a cold sweat at night, then you must recognize that you have an impending problem. Whenever that indelible line is crossed, you cannot turn a blind eye to potentially inappropriate behavior.

There are periods during which any business relationship can enter a gray area. But getting a warning signal does not necessarily mean that you have to fire the customer. You should instead schedule a meeting to probe for honest answers. To prepare for this meeting, have all your facts together and avoid allegations of "he said, she said," as well as glittering generalities. You must be specific as to what transpired that precipitated your angst. After the review is completed, you must be fully prepared to walk or—depending on what you learn—run away from the customer.

Sometimes this is more easily said than done, particularly when you have to deal with meeting payroll and paying your bills. However, you remember the saying, "You'll have to either pay now or pay later." If you make an exception because the customer in question only *occasionally* crosses your ethics line, the long-term cost of the infractions might be much more detrimental than you ever fathomed. On the other hand, taking your concerns to a customer might lead to an understanding that allows you to continue the relationship—and in some cases, not only solidify it, but improve it.

We created a policy on my watch at OfficeMax that provided that vendors could not entertain our employees other than by buying them lunch or a dinner during which business was the main topic. We promulgated this policy to employees and vendors, and required that both acknowledge that they agreed to this policy by signing a form and returning it to us.

Many of the industry conferences and trade shows and conventions where buyers met vendors took place in the original "Sin City," Las Vegas. That actually made good sense, because Vegas had the biggest and best facilities, as well as hotels to fit every travel budget, from posh palaces to places with just a hot shower and clean bed. One of the negatives of this entertainment and business-gathering mecca is that it is a city of excesses. There's just about too much of everything. You name it, and Vegas probably has it.

We not-so-subtly reminded our people before each major event of our lunch and dinner policy. But as there is with every policy, there are those who either push the envelope or blatantly step over the line.

In a combination of both of these, one indiscreet employee was seen leaving—of all places—a Vegas machine-gun shooting range/bar/strip joint with members of a vendor team doing business with the company.

His extremely ill-timed exit from this "entertainment facility" was observed by a senior OfficeMax executive (not me), who was clearly taken aback by what he witnessed. He happened to notice that the members of this particular group were not exactly walking in a straight line, and were also talking loudly, much akin to those who may have had one too many.

Of course, the company could not nor should it tell people where they could hang out and with whom, only that vendors could not pick up the tab. But in this situation, there was at least enough circumstantial evidence to look a little deeper.

The executive who made the sighting (and I never quite understood what he was doing in that area, but that is another story) reported what he saw to our security department, which we called Loss Prevention (LP). This was the team charged with monitoring all policies and looking into matters by using discretion so as not to falsely accuse anyone. Once our LP group was made responsible for investigating this event, they did some checking and found that the charges made at this unique facility were, in fact, paid for with a credit card from the vendor. There was no record that our employee paid his own way.

Our next step was to talk to the employee and let him know that an executive from our team saw him leaving this establishment with vendors. He was asked point-blank if the vendor paid.

He nervously mumbled a no. He was asked to repeat his answer, this time for the formal record. His revised answer was "I don't remember."

The next step was to call the vendor and request that it ask its employees about this event and if it was turned in as a business entertainment expense naming someone from Office-Max as the guest.

The end of the story was that we fired the employee and, when the vendor sheepishly admitted that our policy—to which it had agreed—was stretched to include drinks and use of a machine gun at this shooting range, we enforced our policy and ceased doing business with the vendor.

As an aside, we most likely would not have fired the employee had he been up front when first asked about the violation. We let him go for one simple reason: We assumed that if he lied once, he'd more than likely lie again. As for the vendor, we could not afford to have merchandise sources break a rule that was put in place for obvious reasons that everyone should understand. Our buyers purchased tens of millions of dollars' worth of goods from any one vendor, and where there is smoke there could be fire, and we as a company could get badly burned.

Sometimes, it can be even trickier to fire a customer than to fire a vendor or employee. I was notified in one situation that a key customer was making demands that included tickets for certain events and special consideration for personal discounts. I recommended that we not do business under these circumstances; therefore, we had little to lose by calling the purchasing agent's boss.

So we did—but the boss didn't want to rock the corporate boat by confronting the purchasing agent. We felt we had done all we could, so we fired the customer. We did it professionally but expeditiously, and we walked away from a fair amount of revenue that we thought ultimately would produce a huge amount of problems.

The best way to do business in today's environment is to maintain transparency in the relationship. This significantly helps to avoid unpleasant surprises, and also makes for a more satisfying and longer-term partnership with your customers. This criterion will set the right example for your employees and also lead to a more productive and successful company. As an added plus, you might actually sleep through the night every once in a while.

33

Lesson #33:
Spurring Growth—
How to Eat an Elephant
One Bite at a Time

WHAT DO EATING an elephant and building a business have in common? You do both in the same way—one bite at a time.

One of the biggest challenges when you're building a business is figuring out how to approach that growth. Executives with common sense who are aware of their own vulnerability have all had that sinking feeling in the pit of their stomachs at least once. It occurs when they suddenly become overwhelmed by the size and scope of a pending undertaking that is designed to take their company to the next level. And here you thought getting the company up and running was the hard part!

To get started with one of the bigger meals of your career, you first need to have the idea and conjure up a big picture of what has to be done. It's a lot like what occurs in photography; when you pull back to get the entire subject in the frame, it always looks more daunting than it really is. But once you get the picture in focus and zoom in on the subject, you start to crystallize the individual pieces and parts—but not the entire elephant. You need a close-up of each cross section or smaller piece to launch the development process.

When a project is conceptualized, it typically incorporates all the bells and whistles. From there you rationalize the undertaking—not only economically but also in terms of the time and resources needed to get the job done. But you must answer these questions before you put pencil to paper: When the new initiative, next store, factory, phase of a project, or subsidiary is up and running, will it produce as promised and satisfy the return on investment criterion? Will whatever task you've undertaken serve the end users by offering something special that they will want and need? Once you answer these questions satisfactorily, you're ready to get rolling.

Okay, that sounds simple enough. But what do you do once you have the big picture, know the returns, and have satisfied yourself that it is worth the pain and strain to complete the effort?

The next step is where the "one bite at a time" proverb really comes into play. If you pull back and look only at the big picture, you are likely to be so riddled with second thoughts—and possibly overcome with fear of failure—that you will put this well-conceived effort on the back burner . . . or, worse yet, scrap the idea altogether.

Success is often based on determining which piece to start on first. Logic would suggest starting at the bottom with the foundation, then building up step-by-step. Although this makes sense, sometimes taking the traditional route is not the most efficient, nor the most effective.

Creating something is not always a linear process. You can often start eating that elephant simultaneously from the top, bottom, and middle, with different teams focusing on various tasks. It may be more economical to begin with the middle or end parts for a variety of good reasons, such as the immediate availability of specialized resources or materials.

Here's an example. When opening stores, teams are assigned specific aspects of the project, such as designing the building, laying out the interior, buying the merchandise, creating the grand opening ad campaign, and so forth—with each team doing its own thing concurrently. In the final stages, it takes only a few days or about a week for the fixtures, merchandising, and marketing dots to be connected. When they are, the doors are unlocked and management prays that because it was built, customers will come.

We faced a similar situation after we opened our first OfficeMax location. We knew that we needed three stores to establish a base in our initial test market of Cleveland before we could consider expanding elsewhere. Our eventual goal was to develop a national chain of office supply stores, but we understood that we had to work methodically, putting it together one piece at a time, in order to achieve this seemingly improbable goal.

It all came together on November 4, 1988. We ran our first major promotion to formally launch OfficeMax—a triple grand opening boldly proclaiming in the headline of a double truck ad (two adjoining newspaper pages without what is known as a gutter between the two pages): "Hello, Cleveland, office supply prices just dropped 50%. OfficeMax is here!" This grand opening ad, which I still have, ran on a Sunday in the only Cleveland daily paper, the *Plain Dealer*. I didn't sleep much the night before the opening—but then again, sleeping was a luxury for which I had no time in those early days.

My first stop was our flagship store, Golden Gate, on the east side of Cleveland. As I pulled into the shopping center, I saw a crowd of people and two police cars. Though I initially panicked and wondered what disaster might have occurred, I was pleasantly surprised to find that all those people were there for OfficeMax's opening.

Later that day, many of our investors came to that location and saw the action—along with the fact that our promises had been turned into a reality. After visiting store number one, I drove to the other two stores—and immediately felt as though I had died and gone to heaven. I saw the same phenomenon taking place as I pulled up to each of the other stores—lots of customers and even traffic jams. It doesn't get much better than that in retail.

As day turned to night on that special Sunday, we knew we had something exceptional. The crowds told us, the numbers told us, and everything just felt right. That night, I started working on plans for phase two of OfficeMax: accelerating our expansion.

I knew we needed more money and bigger offices, and because so many of our initial investors could see for themselves the success we had created, it was relatively easy to raise more capital. We called a special investor meeting a few weeks later. As we explained what was coming next and why investors should pony up with more cash to double down their bets and avoid dilution, all of a sudden someone started chanting, "OfficeMax! OfficeMax!"

There is nothing that beats hearing that kind of enthusiasm from a member of your team—nothing.

The key to creating demand is to manage the availability of whatever you're selling. A scarcity of a product or service increases the price and provides a sense of urgency for the buyer. Because we used this strategy in our second round of financing, people predictably started writing checks—some in the very meeting where we announced the new offering.

We also increased the price of this offering, because we'd moved from a theoretical development stage company to a real business that had customers and sales. We bumped the offering from the original $50 a unit to $87.50, which provided a nice step up in the investments. Just about all of the existing investors covered their positions and invested more money, which gave us enough capital to get through the spring and continue our build-out of the chain one store at a time.

We moved our headquarters to a 10,000-square-foot office building in another Cleveland suburb, and opened subsequent stores in Buffalo, New York, and in Detroit, Michigan. These took us outside of the northeast Ohio region and began our national expansion.

The key to this next growth spurt was to make sure that everyone involved had seen the picture of what we were about to undertake. To eat the entire elephant, everyone involved has to know what it is supposed to look like when it's done, even though each person only needs to focus on taking one bite at a time.

And you can't have any illusions. I guarantee that you'll have some indigestion while eating your elephant. No worries, though; that's what Rolaids are for.

34

Lesson #34:
If You Don't Like the
Competition . . . Buy
Them If You Can

COMPETITION SUCKS. I know that doesn't sound politically correct or congenial, but the fact is that either you're gunning for them or they're gunning for you. And like it or not, your competition will probably find some way to exploit your weaknesses if you don't pay attention to them.

We faced a series of hurdles shortly after we survived the milestone first year of OfficeMax during the summer and fall of 1989. Competition was heating up, and we feared that the other operators would begin to move into our markets. It was time to start seriously developing Plan B and ask ourselves: What would we do to preserve the equity value and our precious cash if things went south? My primary task was to ensure that we had enough money, so we raised another round of capital later that year. We more than doubled the price to $200 a share and secured additional investors.

While we were completing this $5 million private placement—our third in just over a year—I received a call from the then-chief financial officer (CFO) of now long-gone Montgomery Ward, which was run by Bernie Brennan at the time. Montgomery Ward had invested $20 million into another office supply super-store chain, Office World, which had seven stores in the metro Chicago area. They had lost $13 million on the initiative and were still sitting on $7 million.

At this point, OfficeMax was operating about 15 stores in four states. We had been receiving a lot of positive press, and gaining market share because of decent execution and gutsy marketing. Chicago was a likely expansion market, and Montgomery Ward recognized this. When the chief financial officer called, he asked if I would come to Chicago and meet with him and Brennan.

During the meeting, Brennan explained why Montgomery Ward had invested in Office World. It didn't make much sense; he was merely trying to find use for the excessive space in his outdated department stores. The problem was that its dingy, cavernous stores served two different customer demographic segments—the low-middle for Ward's and business types for the other. Brennan then made me an offer: Since we weren't direct competitors, he would pay us a huge fee to tell him what was wrong with his office supply chain.

It was a good offer. I thought for a moment and realized I already knew why Office World was an unsuccessful venture. I said, "If you double the amount, I'll tell you what's wrong before I leave the room."

With a skeptical smirk, Brennan said, "Okay. What's our problem?"

"It's simple," I said. "Someone who picked the Chicago locations must have skipped the class on geography."

I went on to explain that the key to success in a retail start-up was having the people making the business decisions close to the customer. Then I detailed how I did my walk-around at OfficeMax stores almost every work night and on the weekends as well. I informed him that his problem was simple to fix. All he had to do was move the corporate offices with all the buyers and decision makers from New York City to where Office World was headquartered: Chicago.

This translated into about 400 reasons—measured in miles— why Montgomery Ward's office supply business was failing. They weren't listening to their customers, because they did not see them every day. Their problem was simple geography: where the stores were located versus where the people running them were located. I further explained that they needed to be much more hands-on and get closer to the customers in order to understand what they needed and wanted.

I left—without the huge fee for my suggested solution—but Brennan said it might make sense for us to buy him out and take over Office World. We started negotiating, not only with Ward, but also with a large venture capital firm, NEA, which owned a big piece of Office World, and GE Capital, which owned Montgomery Ward. They offered to give us the Office World stores, plus the $7 million they hadn't wasted from their original $20 million investment. In exchange, they wanted to own 50 percent of the new company, which would be branded as OfficeMax.

Several of the key players came to Cleveland to meet. I sat in our conference room with my then OfficeMax partner, trying to cut a deal that would take us from 15 stores to more than 20 in one move. My partner was panicking because he knew this could be a make-or-break deal for our growth, especially with the cash infusion.

But I wasn't about to give up half the company. I told them we would give them 20 percent—take it or leave it. If there was no deal, we would enter the Chicago market on our own. And on top of that, we wanted new money—about $5 million.

They wouldn't budge.

"No deal," I said. "I think we're done here. We'll see you soon in Chicago as we become your worst nightmare as your new competitor."

After they left, my partner turned to me and said, "You just ruined this company. We needed that money."

I shook my head. "I'll bet you half your share of the company that they'll call us and cave in before they take off in their fancy company plane."

No more than 30 minutes later, our phone rang. It was Ray Bank, whose family started clothing chain and catalog retailer Jos. A. Bank. Ray worked with NEA, and became a member of the OfficeMax board years later after I took it public. He told me, "Michael, you're a real SOB with ice water instead of blood in your veins, but we want you to become our SOB. We can't afford to take the chance and have to fight with you, so we'll take the deal on your terms."

I told my partner what Ray had said, and he just looked at me and walked out of the room.

Because of the deal—which closed just around our second anniversary in April 1990—we jumped from number 19 to about number 12 in the industry. We suddenly had a strong Midwest focus, improved our buying power, gained more leverage with real estate developers, and sharpened our competitive edge on a number of important fronts.

A word of warning: It is unlikely that you'll always win when you play hardball. Sometimes, if you push *too* hard, your opponent will start coming up with more and more reasons not to give in—because he might feel as though you're challenging his wisdom. This comes with the territory, and you need to be prepared for the occasional setback. I've found in reflecting on the many deals I have done over the years that the net effect is that I've won way more than I've lost—and the ones I *did* win by playing hardball came with huge payoffs. Much of this simply gets down to developing your own style and remembering that one size does not fit all.

35

Lesson #35:
The Easiest Path to
Hypergrowth Is with Other
People's Money

THERE ARE MANY ways to build a company—organic growth through profits reinvested in the company; organic growth through capital injections from investors; and acquisition. But no matter which method you choose, the easiest path to accelerated growth is always on someone else's dime, which I call OPM, or other people's money.

Taking other people's money to fuel expansion doesn't always mean that you'll lose control of your company. A truly savvy entrepreneur can craft smart deals that inject capital, which can be used for rapid expansion, and at the same time maintain control of his or her company.

We knew we weren't finished with acquisitions after we'd expanded OfficeMax through the Office World acquisition. Six months later, in mid-1990, Kmart decided to start its own office supply chain, Office Square, and opened its first stores in our backyard—Canton, Ohio. Worse yet, Kmart CEO Joe Antonini committed tens of millions to getting the venture off the ground.

By this time, Staples and Office Depot were quickly becoming the big dogs in the office supply superstore industry and snapping up smaller competitors at a breakneck pace. I had a little nagging voice in my head that kept saying we needed to step up our efforts and do something about this potentially dangerous competitor. Office Square's presence was intimidating not because they were any good, but because their parent company provided them with much more money than we had. That alone could make them lethal.

So I decided to call Kmart, even though I wasn't quite sure what I would do once I'd reached the CEO. I knew I had to attempt to figure out what was going on with Kmart's business and find out its plans. I assumed that Antonini—just like that girl I didn't know well whom I called when I was 16—would hang up on me. Nevertheless, I knew I still had to try.

It took me a while, but I found someone who had his private phone number and gave him a ring. It was a Tuesday night around 7 PM, and he answered.

"Antonini," he said.

Not knowing quite what to say because I was only prepared for him to hang up on me, I simply responded in kind by saying, "Feuer."

There was a momentary silence before Antonini broke it. "Well, Mr. Feuer," he said. "What can I do for you?"

He knew who I was because we also had stores in Kmart's own backyard of Detroit. I knew he had probably been in our stores and that this conversation would get interesting very quickly because I had made it past the first hurdle—he didn't hang up.

"Well, Mr. Antonini," I said. "I'd like to buy your company."

"Which company?" he asked.

I have a dry sense of humor, so I said, "I don't care—whichever one you want to sell." At that time, Kmart owned numerous brands—Pace, a major wholesale club; Borders; Builders Square, a wannabe Home Depot; and Sports Authority, among many others.

"I'll even buy your office supply company, our competitor, Office Square," I asserted boldly, while I was shaking in my boots.

Antonini laughed. "To tell you the truth, we're not interested," he said. "But I'll take your name and number."

It could have ended there, but I had done my homework. I knew that Kmart was having major problems with the office superstore business. So I wasn't surprised when, a week later, Antonini called me back and asked if I would come up to Detroit for a chat.

When I arrived, I was ushered into the large conference room that reminded me of a room you would expect to see at the United Nations; it was even bigger than the room at Montgomery Ward. It was me, Antonini, and 20 of his closest advisers. After I sat down, he jumped right in.

"Why should I sell you my company?" he asked. "And what can Kmart do for you?"

I was thinking of giving the socially acceptable answer: "It's because of your brilliant strategy, your real estate, your depth of management." But that's never worked for me, so I said, "Well, Joe—if I may call you Joe—I'll tell you the truth. It's your money. That's what we need to do something big. So I'd like you to buy a stake in OfficeMax and also give us your office supply stores with a pile of money to boot."

And what do you know? It worked.

By the time we left that room, we had made a handshake deal—a gigantic one for OfficeMax, valued at $38 million. We wound up getting five of the stores Antonini had opened, in our backyard in northeast Ohio, and Kmart invested about $20 million in new money. As a result, Kmart owned 22 percent of the now larger OfficeMax entity and received one board seat, but we were guaranteed that we would run our own show. I seldom called Kmart after the deal closed and didn't initiate talks with them, because I already had what I wanted—control and the ability to continue to grow OfficeMax by using Kmart's money.

Kmart would call periodically to tell us that they never heard from us—but the reality was that they really didn't care. Our numbers were good, which was great for Kmart. As a result, I was invited up to Detroit a number of times to talk to the Kmart board as a group and sometimes in one-on-one meetings with key individual members. I started to give them my theories on business and why we were succeeding at OfficeMax. Because of this, they took a liking to me. We actually established a very nice relationship.

Then, about four months later, the biggest player in the industry—Office Depot—came calling. They made an offer of about $200 million to buy us out, and my partner wanted to take the money and run. I had a decision to make. I would have made tens of millions with this deal personally if I cashed out—not too bad for a couple of years of hard work. But I also saw the opportunity of taking OfficeMax to a much higher level. Therefore, I went up to Detroit and met with Joe Antonini again.

I explained, "I have a new paradigm that will make you look like a genius. You buy about 90 percent of OfficeMax; we'll keep the rest. You'll buy out all my investors at a huge return on their investment in a very short period of time." I also explained that I was going to cash out half my chips and receive about half my stake in cash. I figured that if I ever had to take any crap from these people, I would just leave without having to worry about money again.

Joe liked the idea and we made the deal. Our shareholders loved us.

Unfortunately, the shine didn't last too long though. Shortly thereafter, Kmart started to get into trouble due to a combination of bad investments it had made and the start of a gradual devaluation of its own core brand chain. Antonini was taking heat from his board. And then there was me, this kid from Cleveland, hanging out with the big dogs on the board on a regular basis.

One day a lead Kmart board member called me and said, "Mike, we would like you to consider coming in as president of all Kmart. We'd like you to spend six months with Joe Antonini and then, when he was ready to pack it in, you'd be his successor. We'll buy out your share of OfficeMax and give you around $40 million. But you'll have to move to Detroit or we'll give you a plane and fly you back and forth from Cleveland every day."

It was, of course, incredibly flattering. However, the behind-the-scenes dealing that would have pushed Antonini out bothered me; he had been my biggest supporter, and I didn't like the Kmart's bureaucracy. Even though I knew I wasn't going to accept the offer, I did take time to think about it. It was almost surreal to be going from nothing on my personal $20,000 investment to tens of millions in just a couple of years. But it just wasn't me, and the situation didn't feel right. So I went back to the Kmart board and told them that I not only didn't want the Kmart job; I also wanted a divorce.

My proposal was to take OfficeMax public and pay Kmart back. The price tag for our freedom was about $625 million by then. When we made our first deal, Antonini had told me that if I needed anything I should just call, and I never called unless I needed money. Among the calls I did make was one asking to buy a chain about as big as us, BizMart (using about $275 million of Kmart's money). I also used Kmart's money to acquire a stake in a company called Corporate Express, as well as Office Warehouse.

Because of my unorthodox yet seemingly effective skills, I'd earned a good reputation with Kmart execs. They were impressed with how I'd taken the small retail chain and built it into a large player. Kmart was also coming unraveled at the seams with problems at every turn. So they bought into my idea.

In November 1994 we went public in the largest IPO of any retail chain to that date and paid Kmart back every penny. They kept a 22 percent stake, but three months later, we did a secondary offering and sold those shares to the public, as well. In the end, Kmart got back its original money and made a handsome return on its investment in OfficeMax that approached $1 billion. At the same time, we had managed to build OfficeMax into one of the largest companies in the industry by using one of my favorite sources—OPM, or other people's money.

36

Lesson #36:
Beating the Competition Requires That You Know More about Their Vulnerabilities Than They Know about Themselves . . . And Knowing Yourself Better Than They Know You

POLITICIANS AND CEOs alike always talk about competition being a good thing, which is really only partially correct. Sure, having others in the same sandbox makes you keeping thinking, testing, and improving. But in reality too much competition in the early stages of a start-up can cause a lot of pain and suffering, and—if you're not careful—might prove fatal.

In the early stages of OfficeMax, particularly the first year or so, we scrupulously stayed away from competitors. Were we afraid of a good fight? No. But we wanted to pick a time and place of our choosing for it. The industry's 800-pound gorillas—including Staples and Office Depot—seemed to carve out imaginary regions of the country as their then-exclusive domains. This gave us (and probably the others) some time to fine-tune and work out the kinks—everything from training, merchandise assortments, and marketing messages to figuring out what the customers really wanted.

Staples started in the Boston area and stayed in New England during the first couple of years. Office Depot began in south Florida and remained in the South. And OfficeMax began in Cleveland and initially stuck to the Rust Belt.

In our first-phase expansion, we hovered within a 300-mile radius of our home base's sanctuary. The reality was that before we had access to Kmart's deep pockets, we could not afford too many potentially mean-spirited, competitive fights in those first few years.

My theory then—as well as now—is that it is dangerous to jump into a fight, especially when you choose to pick on anyone your size and definitely someone bigger than you. I don't like fair fights, because they imply no better than a 50/50 chance of winning. I don't like being the underdog. It sounds macho to take others on, but the odds don't work for me.

There were numerous reasons for avoiding competition other than those I've already cited. One is that the ability to gain quick market share and customer acceptance improves significantly when a company can play aggressive offensive ball versus implementing a defensive posture. Usually, the player with the bigger guns and most bullets wins. So when you don't have much of either, it's smart to simply avoid fights in the first place.

Our plan at OfficeMax was to stay in the shadows and play an "aw-shucks" game, so we didn't become a threat for the big guys. We wanted them to think, "How threatening could these Midwesterners possibly be? If they were any good, they would come play in the big leagues with us." But our plan was to do the honorable thing and pick on the small guy who was gouging the customer.

The small operators were doing business in a way that was convenient for them: Their store hours were when they wanted to be open, not necessarily when the customer wanted to shop. They also levied the highest possible price rather than charging fairly and providing value-added benefits to the customer. This made for easy pickings because the customer almost immediately got it and switched to OfficeMax.

This lack of competition during our early days was a godsend, as it enabled us to fine-tune our concept. However, as it is often said, "All good things must come to an end." As sure as God made little green apples, the competition came.

We didn't feel sheer panic when that first occurred; however, the new competition did make for more than a few occasionally restless nights. But this sensation—that uneasy feeling in the gut—was short-lived. As the kids say, "It is what it is." The truth was that we had been on a gravy train, picking off the little guys without worrying about real competitors. Once the competition showed up, we had to figure out how to play real hardball. That meant learning more about our competitors than they knew about themselves, as well as knowing ourselves better than they could possibly know us.

This real-life game of Gladiator required us to become even more customer-centric. Our mantra was that we needed to look at the business through the customers' eyes for whatever we did, and see what was in it for them. Examples of this included changing our store hours from an early 8 AM opening time to an even earlier 7 AM in certain markets where small business owners did their own shopping and needed to start their day sooner.

I am actually a huge proponent of competition today, particularly in industries where I have no economic stake. That's not selfish; it's more a case of human nature. Simply put, competition makes companies better—despite the fact that the learning process can be painful. Much like lifting weights and exercising, the reality is as the coaches tell us: "No pain, no gain."

I religiously watched the competition during those early days, and every year thereafter. Every Monday morning for about 15 years we would have an all-hands meeting that included all of our key executives—as well as the managers who actually had to act on the decisions we made in these meetings. We prided ourselves on the ability to make changes immediately and initiate new processes and programs. We also felt that we were always ready to change something that was obviously not working without requiring a dozen meetings to discuss it and act on it. The customer was always the driver—and giving customers what they wanted and needed even before they realized it was always our primary goal.

These meetings were meant to serve as a review of the past week, with a major focus on the competition. We literally looked at every competitor's ad that ran throughout the United States, and dissected the content, pricing, and approach. As a follow-up to that, we made it mandatory that every product manager or buyer—whom we called category managers—pay a weekly visit to the competition. We broke up the team into groups so that we could cover the entire country. We used a private jet, and I— along with other members of management—went out at least one day a week during peak seasons and traveled from market to market.

Our policy was that we had to fill every seat when we used the jet. We often took a junior person along with us just to give them the experience and us the opportunity to get to know up-and-comers better. And whenever we visited the competition, we also visited our own stores—just to learn a little more about ourselves.

Interestingly enough, the store employees always knew when we were coming. I finally figured out that the district managers had somehow been bribing the travel people or administrative assistants to find out when and where we were heading on these surveillance missions. I found this particularly annoying because the store employees who found out that we were coming in advance would pull an all-nighter, scrub the floors, and make the stores perfect.

I finally broke people of this habit. As commander-in-chief of OfficeMax Air Force One, many times we would take off heading for one city, and I would go to the pilot in midflight and change the city we were visiting next. Within an hour, we would be somewhere where no one was expecting us. This provided us with both a tremendous revelation and a heavy dose of reality.

The district and store managers in the cities that were expecting us spent all day waiting for our "surprise appearance" that never came. A side benefit was the stores got a quick and thorough scrub from top to bottom. Conversely, the district managers in the cities to which we made the secret visits were scrambling to get to the location while we were still there. Many times we found some atrocious situations; other times we were ecstatically surprised with how fantastic the stores looked. This, too, became a way of doing business at OfficeMax, and we operated in this kind of "stealth mode" for years.

I had a simple protocol when I went to every OfficeMax store. I would enter, announce who I was (even though most people recognized me), and then, before leaving, I would walk every square foot, aisle by aisle. I would ask a sales associate to accompany me as I walked and tell me what their customers were telling them.

I would frequently ask the manager to walk with other people in my entourage so I could learn more from the lower-level associates. This experience was especially interesting because people who worked at that level really did tell me what they thought without much regard to wondering what I wanted to hear.

I viewed these types of visits as low-hanging fruit because they were much cheaper—and much more fun—than market research, which always lost something in the translation. I would always send a letter to the stores after visiting to thank them for the hospitality and find at least something good to say (which was occasionally difficult). I would also write another memo to the district manager that—in unemotional and incredibly candid terms—would spell out the good, the not so good, and the terrible. I would then ask them to produce a plan with time and action measures to correct shortcomings.

I followed the same procedure of introducing myself to the manager when visiting a competitor. I found that when I was up-front about who I was and stated that I had great respect for the competitor's operation, the manager would open up. The manager would tell me things about his specific store that made me shudder to think that our people might be doing the same. But I didn't have any illusions that they weren't.

I learned a lot from these competitor visits, and the best lesson that I still use today is, "If you don't ask, you'll never get." I would frequently receive phone calls from my counterpart CEOs at the other companies, who would ask somewhat sarcastically, "How did the store look?"

I would also reply, "You're so damn good, it's amazing we're still in business."

This always produced a muffled laugh.

I also assumed that the competitors' executives made the same visits to our stores, and we established a policy as to how to handle the visits and what to tell them. Some of our more creative people no doubt mastered the technique of disinformation, a concept that is included in most spy novels. I believe in having fun while working and turned a blind eye to this activity.

One of my favorite TV shows years ago was *The X-Files*, mostly because each show would begin with the declaration: "The Truth Is Out There." And as a CEO, the trick is finding it.

37

Lesson #37:
If You Negotiate with Yourself, You Have a Fool for an Opponent

DURING MY CAREER I have been the primary negotiator on thousands of transactions—from store leases to vendor contracts to major acquisitions and just about everything in between. A deal is much like a love story. At the beginning, both parties have great expectations; in the middle, everybody reaches the frustration point; and then there is a happy ending—boy gets girl, or, in a business deal, handshakes and high-fives abound.

The best deals are when both sides feel they won, and that they outsmarted, outmaneuvered, or got the better of the other guy. This is basically human nature, as there seems to be an insatiable need deep down inside to secretly believe that although it's called a win–win deal, your side prevailed at the expense of the other camp.

And just as a boxer trains for a big fight, there are specific steps that I take before ever sitting down at the negotiation table.

I first undertake a cerebral process in which I complete something that I call a *deal inventory* by asking myself the following questions: "Do I really want to do this thing?" "Am I sure that whatever I'm trying to negotiate adds value and it is not just about winning?" And before I even start, I identify the point at which I am prepared to say, "Thanks, but no thanks," and walk away.

Make no mistake about it—there are many theatrics in the negotiating process. Some people like to play the tough guy, others the country bumpkin, and a few portray utter indifference. You have to prepare the persona you want to exhibit and pick the best costume for the circumstances to create your character.

You must also find out everything there is to know about the opponent. Talk to people who know the person's style of doing business. If applicable, research past trigger points that the person used in other transactions. You can do this by studying previous news reports or by talking to someone who knew someone else involved in prior undertakings. People love to tell their professional war stories; it's often just a matter of picking up the phone and asking the right questions.

Decide on the first meeting place. Although this sounds simple and might cause you to say, "Who cares?" my answer is that *you* must care. You might want to let the opponent meet at his or her office. Why? Well, if you invite someone to your home, you're going to normally act like the gracious host—someone who's less likely to be contentious. On the other hand, you may want to try for home court advantage and control the environment by meeting in your office.

The first session for bigger deals typically takes place in neutral territory—either a banker's office or a quiet restaurant. It's important to always sit with your back to the wall in an eatery; if your opponent has that power seat, you'll lose your concentration as you watch him observe who is coming and going. Try to meet one-on-one; this will allow you to avoid having your opponent waste time as he tries to impress whomever he brought along with his or her superior bargaining skills. Equally important, be sure the person with whom you're meeting has the juice to do the deal and is not just someone "carrying the mail" and relaying messages.

Sooner or later, it's time to get down to business. Force the other side to make the opening offer whenever possible, and remember that sometimes it is what you *don't* say that matters most. We have all heard of a seller offering a price range; for example, someone selling a car offers "between $10,000 and $12,000." No one in his or her right mind is going to jump at the higher price. Let the other person show his or her cards first.

Pay attention to body language as well, because this plays an important role in understanding the negotiation dynamics. There are always signs that provide clues to what the other person is thinking—moisture at the hairline (anxiety), the thumping of fingers (impatience), and the Adam's apple bobbing (panic). Almost everyone has habits of one sort or another that we display when we engage in stressful discussions. I always try to create a mental road map of how someone responds to questions. It could be something as simple as the opponent tugging on his or her ear when thinking about giving in on a point. You learn by noting how the person acted—or in this case, tugged—just before saying during an earlier meeting, "Okay, I'll give you that."

It's equally important to keep your own little inclination-revealing signals in check. Don't fool yourself; we all have them.

If you don't know what your signals are, ask a significant other, your assistant, or a peer.

And always—be patient. Transactions take time, and you have to let them play out. It shows when you are overly eager, and you end up paying more as the buyer and getting less as the seller. I have used other techniques—such as being late for a session or not showing at all and sending a stand-in—that inevitably resulted in the other side fixating on what my lateness or absence meant. Of course, I'd always call to apologize with a good excuse. In many cases, this prompted my opponents to take their eyes off the ball and the important deal points. In a few transactions, the other side walked away—sometimes for a few weeks, one time for as long as a year. You always want to leave the door open when the talking stops; however, you also have to realize when you're at the end of the road. Making a deal for the sake of "just doing it" can be costly and painful.

One critical component of deal-making is to never make a promise you can't or don't intend to keep. Under no circumstances should you *ever* offer something you are not prepared to give. I have seen some negotiations that start out with a promise or two to loosen up the other side, knowing full well it would be reneged on later. This is a bad move. Disingenuous actions will cause someone to be labeled as an unreliable blowhard. You need to say it and stick with it to quickly build credibility.

What are most important are the things you *don't* say; these can mean the difference between closing a deal and one that goes nowhere. I have been in talks where the other guy was negotiating with himself. He was asking the questions, and then answering them before I could open my mouth. Not only is that a time waster, it's superfluous and an exercise in futility. Asking numerous repetitive rhetorical questions will thrust you into a vicious cycle on a road to nowhere. It's much like playing ping-pong with yourself—there is never a winner in either case.

We all engage in this exasperating process from time to time. However, when negotiating with yourself becomes a habitual routine, you're well on your way to diluting your effectiveness and becoming imprudent.

Do not confuse negative mental gymnastics—asking questions for the sake of questions—with the more productive process of playing "What if?" games. The difference is that posing "What if?" questions about relevant matters—to both yourself and others—can be an effective tool. If you use a series of facts to which you can add various suppositions to predict the most likely outcomes, you can move a process forward. Without the facts, however, you will wear yourself out playing these "What if?" games and have nothing to show for your efforts except frustration.

Negotiating with yourself can migrate from the subconscious to the conscious—and then erupt into a full-fledged traumatic episode. After submitting your proposal, and before you receive any feedback, you conjure up responses that you think you might receive, and then engage in a second-guessing game of woulda, coulda, shoulda. In essence, you can predict with relative certainty how the other side will respond in the majority of situations.

By way of an example, let's examine the key factors in a typical acquisition by one company of another. Company A decides to buy Company B because there are management, market, and/or economic synergies. Company A makes its offer and the decision usually gets down to three fundamental considerations: First, what is the price? Is it fair or a lowball offer? Moreover, who gets how much and when? Second, which side will get to call the shots in the newly configured venture at the end of the day? Combining management teams by calling it a "merger of equals" and attempting to keep everybody happy is about as likely as winning the lottery. Although it might sound great in theory, the desired results are usually nothing more than a PR spin based on fairy tales. Third, which side will be perceived as the winner in the public's eye? This is particularly significant in public company transactions. You always want to keep these types of predicable factors in mind because—based on empirical results—they are good antidotes for negotiating with yourself.

There's a simple preventive method that can help you avoid endless self-doubt during the downtime between making your offer and getting your first response. After you fire your salvo in the form of whatever you're offering, stand down and wait until there is something to respond to other than your own self-doubts and negative thoughts. Although it will take a Herculean effort and willpower, refrain from questioning your proposal and always give the other side first opportunity to respond. This will eliminate—or at least, dramatically reduce—your own internalized histrionics. Not only will you be more productive, but you'll be a better leader and possibly a happier executive. Moreover, you'll become a better and smarter negotiator.

Phase Four

The Payday

38

Lesson #38:
Payday . . . And Lessons
from the IPO Road Show

ONE OF THE most exciting—although occasionally frightening—aspects of any business adventure and running a company is not knowing what the future holds or what issues of seemingly gargantuan proportions a CEO will confront. It can be a variety of issues and events—lack of money, incredibly difficult competition, recalcitrant employees, or grim economic conditions. The fact is that the more positive you make the journey—and the more you can gain satisfaction from solving the problems—the less you'll drive yourself to the brink with worry.

However, after a lengthy period of growth and reinvention, the next logical phase for every entrepreneur and his or her team is the payday, which rewards investors, employees, and yourself with some serious folding money. Most entrepreneurs continually reinvest money back into their company as a means for funding it and giving themselves the best chance of establishing something of real value, as well as staving off dilution as others invest alongside the entrepreneur. But there's always a point when the entrepreneur should take money off the table. Deciding exactly when this should be takes a combination of intuition, reading the tea leaves correctly, and realizing—in some cases—when the party might be coming to end. There are always signs pointing the way. The trick is to prepare to make the move before a crisis erupts or the trends turn in the wrong direction—because once that happens, your choices will be limited, and you'll likely jump into the first lifeboat you see.

There are numerous ways for an entrepreneur to create a significant capital event. He or she can cash out by selling all or part of the company to a private equity firm, or selling the 100 percent to a competing or complementary entity. Those who aren't faint of heart can always take a company public through an initial public offering or IPO, provided the financials can support the case to do so.

In my case, I pulled a hat trick—creating three different yet significant capital events with OfficeMax.

The earliest of these took place when Kmart bought its initial stake in the company, and I took my first cut. The second was our IPO. And the last one occurred when I went to the cashier's window in 2003 and sold the entire company to Boise Cascade.

Going public can be a true adventure in itself, sometimes even more daunting than building the organization in the first place. But an IPO provides a great learning experience; it's a once-in-a-lifetime event to get to enter this exclusive club. There's a definite art to doing an IPO, especially when it comes to the proverbial road show that leads up to the first stock trade.

After Kmart agreed to my proposal to spin off OfficeMax and go public, our next step was to pick the lead investment banker that would take us on this arduous journey. Kmart wanted to select the banker; however, I learned a long time ago that picking advisers—be it attorneys, accountants, or bankers—was much like having a dog in that they seldom bite the hand that feeds them. The number-one thing that investment bankers respect is money and it's hard to take on an IPO without a happy CEO. Had I let Kmart pick the bankers, the firms would be beholden to Kmart, and that would not fly with me.

There was an investment banking firm called Donaldson, Lufkin & Jenrette (DLJ for short) in the heyday of the mid-1990s that was subsequently sold in 2000 to the European bank group Credit Suisse. In its day, DLJ was one of the most street-smart, aggressive, and successful bankers in the country, particularly for renegade-type start-ups that were on the verge of creating a major capital event—like going public. The fees in taking a company public are in the tens of millions, and this certainly gets Wall Street firms' attention.

After the typical wrangling and angst (which had become a regular part of my relationship with Kmart), they succumbed to my request and I signed up DLJ as the lead banker, with several other bankers to the right on the prospectus's front page. The pecking order on an IPO looks like this: The lead banker is on the left, the next most powerful on the immediate right, and so forth. The OfficeMax offering also included Morgan Stanley, William Blair & Company, Dean Witter Reynolds, and McDonald & Company. We selected each banker for a specific purpose, either because of its broker network and distribution capabilities or because of its analyst strength. It's important to note that choosing a firm based on an analyst is a no-no nowadays; the ground rules have changed and analysts' independence—which separates them from investment banking clients—makes it a whole new ballgame.

The next step was to determine whether OfficeMax would become an over-the-counter stock, list on NASDAQ, or go to the New York Stock Exchange (NYSE). In the 1990s the New York Stock Exchange had more of a stuffy, blue-blood, white-shoe reputation, while NASDAQ was perceived more as the right home for entrepreneurs. To make the call, I decided to hold a beauty contest and invited both NASDAQ and the NYSE to visit me in Cleveland. The team from NASDAQ showed up, and it immediately became clear to me that they were drinking their own bathwater. They thought they were much better than I thought they really were.

In contrast, a diminutive, five-foot-six-inch, 130-pound executive from the NYSE by the name of Dick Grasso—who was then number two at the Exchange and later went on to become its CEO—showed up at my front door. Dick had the ability to make whomever he was speaking to think they were the most important person in the world or ran the company that mattered most. Dick went through the virtues of the NYSE and—while keeping my cards close to the vest—I told him I would make a decision and call him in one week.

When I arrived at work at 8 AM seven days later, Dick Grasso was waiting in the lobby. He had personally come to get my answer; he was asking for the order, wanted my business, and was not shy about showing he meant it. I showed him into my office and immediately gave the nod for the IPO listing to the NYSE.

A key aspect of taking any company public is packaging the organization for prime time. This fast-paced and sometimes difficult process takes a phenomenal amount of time, energy, concentration, and determination. A bit of showmanship doesn't hurt either. It also can be exceedingly intimidating and utterly frustrating unless the CEO gets ahead of the process.

Fortunately, I had significant experience giving speeches and selling OfficeMax and myself during the previous years. I also represented OfficeMax and Kmart at many Wall Street–type analyst meetings during our time with Kmart. This practice gave me a leg up in the IPO process, which began with a series of rehearsals in New York City.

In essence it goes something like this: The lead banker invites all the other investment bankers, including those from the other firms in the deal, to a big meeting. Management has at it, trying to sell the company during this dry run. Following the presentation, management is then peppered with questions—the more difficult and outrageous the better.

However, after enduring several rehearsals, I finally told the bankers to "bug off." They were confusing me with their advice and I didn't think much of it anyway. I would do it my way, and promised them that it would work.

The next step was preparing for the actual road show, which in this case spanned an incredible almost four weeks—150 different speeches in 20-plus major markets in the United States and then a week of shuttle-jet diplomacy in Europe, making speeches in places such as London, Paris, Edinburgh, and Geneva, all of which after the second day became a blur. The bankers even threw in a few video/teleconference presentations in Asia for good measure, which I did in the middle of the night from my Paris hotel room.

An interesting aspect of the road show for a CEO is that he or she quickly learns that the most difficult aspect of the process is staying "up" and staying compelling. I learned that it was basically acceptable to do just about anything except bore people. So after a few sessions, I developed my own process to stay engaged. I believe that most CEOs simply repeat the same presentation time after time; in essence, the presentation given on day one is the same given on the last day. But I decided to entertain myself by changing each presentation's format, trying to tailor it to the interests of the audience I was addressing. I still connected everything to the story I had to tell, but I altered the sequence and anecdotes to serve my purpose.

Finally, after weeks of travel, presentations, and near-madness, I arrived in New York City on my private jet late on the evening of November 3, 1994, at about 1 AM I was immediately whisked away in a stretch limousine to the Millennium Hotel on Wall Street, a few blocks from the storied New York Stock Exchange. If I hadn't been so exhausted, I probably would have been excited. But at that point, it was just the next step in the process as far as I was concerned. Earlier that day, the senior executives from OfficeMax's headquarters had arrived in New York City, along with my wife, Ellen, who would be with me for the big day.

At about 9:15 AM, we were ushered to the floor of the NYSE, where it was customary for the CEO of a newly listed company to make the first 100-share purchase. The OfficeMax stock had been priced the night before at $19 a share, about $4 above the anticipated price—and now it was showtime.

The first trade by the specialist at the exchange would be based on demand. Because of all the publicity, the strong stock market, and—I like to think—at least somewhat due to how effectively I had sold the company in the 150 meetings, the specialist on the floor of the Exchange assigned to trade our stock could not immediately get the OfficeMax stock opened because there was a dramatic influx of orders. The initial whisper number—a figure at which the specialists think the stock might open—hovered at around $22. The exchange in those days made a practice of trying to open a new stock listing at a price so that it would have some legs and move up during the day.

After about an hour had passed, I started to think this was never going to happen because of the demand for the stock. As we hovered around the specialist trading post on the floor where OfficeMax (OMX) was going to be traded, many traders were screaming bids at the specialist. My wife, Ellen, strayed from the pack and was standing next to several traders. Ellen overheard one of the traders screaming to the specialist, as he raised his bid, "What's OMX do?"

What Ellen quickly learned from this observation was that the momentum traders on the floor sometimes didn't have a clue what the company did—nor did they even care. They simply watched the momentum, purchased a stock when it opened, and would trade it within minutes.

Finally, after about an hour and a half, Dick Grasso informed us that we were ready to move forward. Flashing on the screen above the post was the first trade of OMX at $24 a share—a whopping 25-plus percent above the IPO price. The first few hours OMX was traded on the NYSE were largely another blur in the process, with all of the days now running together. I quickly tired of the theatrics, and just wanted to get back to work. So, following an elaborate lunch with our entourage, we were driven by limo to Teterboro Airport in New Jersey, boarded the private Hawker jet that had been provided by the investment bankers, and flew back to reality. A mere hour and a half later, we landed in Cleveland and were chauffeured back to our headquarters in Shaker Heights, Ohio.

On the way back to the office, I called ahead and asked our human resources vice president to assemble the 800 or so employees in the main building in our auditorium. I felt it was important to share this event with them because of what we had accomplished. I always had—and still have—a reputation of communicating, sometimes to a fault. But I feel that people will do what needs to be done, as long as they know the reasons why. I never miss an opportunity to share the story behind the story with those who need and deserve to know. This engages the team and makes them a part of the process.

When I arrived at the office, I went to the auditorium, where virtually all the employees—from the janitors to the top executives—were assembled. I received a standing ovation as I entered the room, but immediately stopped the thunderous applause by holding up my arms and demanding silence. I made a simple opening statement: "It is I who applauds each and every one of you for making this milestone a reality."

I then started clapping, and everybody joined in. I went on to explain that running a company is "a marathon, not a sprint, and that while today is our day to shine, tomorrow we have to continue to produce results." It was time to give everyone a lesson in the sobering reality of running a public company. I had frequently told this same group that my favorite business book was *The Devil and Daniel Webster*, a short story by Stephen Vincent Benét. In that story, Daniel promises to do whatever the devil asks, which I explained to my employees was akin to a company going public. Now that we had taken the public's money, we had to play by its rules—whether we liked it or not.

The ceremony concluded at about 4:30 PM, and I went to my office to do some real work for about two hours. Then I drove home. I was excited to arrive; I also was physically and emotionally drained. The first thing I did was go on my customary three-mile run, and when I got back home my wife reminded me what day it was and there was something else that had to be done. It was garbage night, and my job—when I was home—was to wheel the garbage can down our 100-yard driveway to the street. So I did it with style and determination, knowing that to succeed, you gotta do what has to be done—at home, at work, and anywhere duty calls.

Beginning November 5, 1994, the world changed for OfficeMax—and for me. For the ensuing nine years I would go on to run OfficeMax as its chairman and CEO before selling it on December 8, 2003, to Boise Cascade for approximately $1.5 billion.

39

Lesson #39:
If the Flame Starts
Flickering: How to Tell If the
Fat Lady Is About to Sing

ONE OF THE biggest dilemmas for any entrepreneur, CEO, or business owner, big or small, is to know when enough is enough. Many times it gets down to the age-old question: Do you work to live or live to work?

Way too many entrepreneurs have worn out their welcome and crashed and burned after reaching a high point, only to precipitously fall from grace in the eyes of those who matter—associates, investors, sometimes customers, and even family. There are many waypoints along the journey to establishing, building, and running a company. An entrepreneur who can come up with a killer idea may not be effective at building on it once its strategy is fleshed out and ready for execution. In other cases, a leader might be a good builder but a failure at running day-to-day operations. The challenge is to understand when it's time to fade to black, and either leave permanently or bring in another executive to run the show—altogether or day-to-day. Perhaps an even more important decision is not whether to wear the hats of innovator, builder, and operator, but instead when to step up to the cashier's window.

There are peaks and valleys in virtually every company and industry. The trick for an owner is to understand these vacillations and know when to hit the bid. This essentially means either accepting an offer to sell and cash out or, in some cases, creating a scenario that results in an offer. This is where one needs to draw the distinction about living to work or working to live. If you fall into the latter bucket, then you're going to have to make some difficult decisions. The greed factor can make things simple and the decision easier. As they say on Wall Street, when a stock has reached the point when everyone wants to own it or buy more, it is probably fully valued and it's best to be a seller. This also applies to selling a business. If, on the other hand, one lives to work, one's energy could be redirected and rechallenged. This might include, for example, creating another business after the existing one has been sold. Even if a company is 100 percent owned by the entrepreneur, he or she still has a moral obligation to provide for all of the organization's constituents. Sometimes the best way to provide is to step out of the picture and give others their day in the sun.

As an entrepreneur, leader, and CEO, I have always been most frightened of the fat lady continuing to sing and sing until she is the only one left who is listening. In this scenario, the show may not be technically over; but it is in reality finished when the audience stops caring or walks under that ubiquitous exit sign. The key to a fulfilling life and continued success is not acquiescence, but knowing how and when to reinvent one's business and even personal life. It's all about looking for that new twist or turn that might ignite a new burning in the belly. To do this, one must remain aware of what is happening around one, and most important, read the subtle signs that something new is in the wind. Things can suddenly change, and you must constantly remain aware of shifts that will give you that next window of opportunity.

Without warning, it can seem as if cold water has inexplicably doused that incessant burning in the gut that awakens overachievers in the morning and gnaws at them until they reluctantly let go and drift off to sleep at night. The search for a better way fuels that constant internal flame. It encourages the most fervent business minds to create a plan on how to one-up the competition or to take one for the team under the sometimes sophomoric assumption that to die figuratively for the company is to live forever.

It happens to just about every entrepreneur: Almost out of the blue, you realize something has changed. At first you probably think it's that virus that's going around. You're lethargic. Your thinking isn't as sharp as it has been. Your mind, for no apparent reason, wanders from ROIs, gross margins, and the bottom line to abstract, granular thoughts—as in white, sandy beaches.

If you're an owner–entrepreneur or top C-level executive who's been stricken by this bug, you initially assume that you're just tired. You rationalize that you'll bounce back like the bull in the china shop, kicking behinds and taking names after a few days away or a couple of good nights' sleep. However, after several extra-long weekends off, you return even more lethargic. Instead of using your steel-trap mind to capture every word, concept, and nuance during meetings, your thoughts drift to unrelated matters. You leave the meeting knowing that if someone put a .45 to your head and said, "Give me a one-minute synopsis of what was discussed or you're toast," you'd reply, "Get the butter and jelly."

What gives? The answer is that the flame is flickering and in the heat of battle, that high thermostat reading just makes you sweat instead of causing your blood to boil. Welcome to Burnout City. It can happen to the best of us—your employees, your friends, and yes—even to you.

The good news is that you can take steps to refocus. You can try to reignite, and if that doesn't work, you can extinguish the flame. Whatever approach you choose, you have to do it your way. You might even be able to have it both ways, depending on where you are in your career, what you're doing, and, most important, what in your life remains undone.

There are some things you can do to try to refan the flames. But the truth is that you'll know it when it's not happening—and when you do, it's time to take that alternative fork in the road and map an exit strategy that leaves the place a little better than when you got there. In business, as in love, it all comes down to dealing with alternatives and making choices—and the end can sometimes be an exciting new beginning. Remember, your work is what you do, not who you are. Many a smoldering fire has reignited into a burning blaze; the flames just needed to be fanned a bit.

That time arrived for me when I decided to sell OfficeMax. The company had been—at least in my mind anyway—something I did for 16 years. I was thrilled that what I did employed about 50,000 people and did business in every state but Vermont, with international operations in China, Japan, Brazil, and Mexico. In addition, it was a company that had its good times and bad. However, at the end of the day, OfficeMax fulfilled its promise of "serving its customers, creating opportunities for its employees, and building value for its shareholders."

While driving to work on one very inauspicious morning in March of 2003, my mind shifted without warning from my train of thought regarding the day's tasks. I began to think instead about my life after OfficeMax, and the lives, so to speak, of my people. I was not in any way tired of the company; business was on a positive upturn, and our outlook was the best it had been in a couple of years. However, as I drove, I started to formulate a rough idea of how I would go about testing the waters to deter-mine if the time was right to either sell the company or merge it with another compatible business that would create a much bigger and more substantial retail juggernaut.

The questions that I asked myself before I pulled into the OfficeMax parking were: If I sold, where could I find a buyer that would pay the best price? And (probably primarily for egocentric reasons) would the name that I created on a legal pad 16 years earlier endure, along with the culture and security for my team? I'm a realist and recognized that the latter two of the three were long shots at best.

I went through my ritual of getting updates on sales from the previous day when I got to my desk that fateful morning, even though I had already seen the top-line numbers three hours earlier as I rolled out of bed and picked up my PDA smartphone. As soon as these tasks were behind me, I told my assistant to cancel all my morning appointments because I needed some quiet time. She could tell I was antsy, so she left quickly and closed the door behind her.

When it is time for thinking, I always pick up my recorder, turn it on, and start talking to it. I vividly recall dictating a surprisingly comprehensive outline of the steps I had to take to test the waters for a merger or sale. Somehow, I had arrived at the conclusion that this was what I needed to do for all concerned.

My thoughts flowed like an open spigot, and I had a plan and a target within an hour. I then called a few merger and acquisition type banker friends and asked them to find out who the investment banker was for the target company, which they accomplished in less than a half hour. As it turned out, I knew the banker at Goldman Sachs that represented my most likely candidate. This made the next step even easier. I made a call to my good friend at McDonald & Company, then owned by KeyBank in Cleveland. As head of investment banking, my friend knew the drill. I explained to him in less than 15 minutes exactly what I wanted him to do. Interestingly, even though he was a close friend and could certainly have asked why I was taking this huge step, he never did and I never offered an explanation.

By noon that day, I had put into motion steps that would permanently change the course of OfficeMax and most likely my life. Even more strangely, I then went about my business for the rest of that day and didn't give my new pursuit another thought.

Around 7 PM that same evening, my banker left me a one-word telephone message that said it all: "Ca-ching." I knew that message meant he had made contact with the other banker and had explained what I wanted to talk about, and that the banker "got it."

My bankers came out to the office and met with me within a few days. I presented them with a pitch paper that outlined the rationale for a deal with my targeted buyer, Boise Cascade, a multimillion-dollar forest products company and operator of Boise Office Products, headquartered in its namesake town in Idaho. On Thursday, April 17, 2003, we left Cleveland for a secret trip to Chicago and a rendezvous with the CEO of Boise and his banker. We kept the meeting hush-hush because both companies were public and I didn't want anyone on my team to know what I had in mind just yet.

Present at the meeting were the CEO of Boise and his Goldman Sachs banker, with whom I had worked previously when OfficeMax acquired BizMart office products. We quickly engaged in a few words of gracious chitchat and thanked each other for the meeting. Then I launched into my pitch as to why a merger or us buying them—or vice versa—made sense. The reasons were easy to understand: We had more than a thousand retail office product stores and Boise had a large contract office supply business selling mostly to Fortune 1,000–type corporations. OfficeMax needed contract stationery in its portfolio to better compete with Office Depot and Staples, the other two survivors of the bloody 15-year office products holy wars.

At that point, the CEO piped up and claimed that the partnership seemed like a natural thing to do. He went on to suggest that one possibility would be for him to run the forestry business, while I managed the office products piece. I immediately made a statement that would set the tone for the next eight months, which was, "I'm America's worst employee, and I'm not working for anyone or sharing the CEO slot." Then, I blurted out, "I hate trees."

To this day, I can't believe I said what I said about trees, because I don't—hate them, that is. I, however, did instantly dislike that CEO. I couldn't put my finger on exactly why at the time, but a sixth sense told me that he and I would eventually "go to the mats," to use a term from the book and the movie *The Godfather*, which signified that the grand fight of all fights was going to take place.

The meeting ended at midnight, and within an hour we were wheels up on our jet back to Cleveland.

Our discussions moved into high gear over the next few weeks—and that was when the chemistry between the other CEO and I went south. This guy just had no sense of humor and took himself way too seriously, and no way was he as smart as he thought he was. His people also seemed to really dislike him, primarily because he was so damn pompous.

In the end, partially because he thought he was smarter than his bankers, the CEO wound up overpaying for OfficeMax because of the unique structure that I developed (that I wasn't even sure I understood at the beginning). And, because the Boise boss could never admit he didn't grasp a difficult concept, he simply got sucked into a deal that went against Boise. The final price was tied to Boise's and our stock prices. We got lucky by catching a wave when the market rallied.

And when it was all over, the other CEO underscored my theory that the best way to lose is by drinking your own bathwater.

On the day our deal closed—December 3, 2003—the combined market value of both companies was almost $3 billion. That value had dropped by more than half—and then continued to fall as the two companies were integrated into one. The newly combined company hit difficult times and management turnover skyrocketed. The Boise CEO left the company, and the newly appointed CEO—a longtime Boise executive—held the office for a short time, before he was forced to hit the bricks by his board. Further, the vast majority of the OfficeMax team who went with the new owners didn't stick around long.

A lot of companies talk about combining a business and making one plus one equal three or more—but it seldom happens. Different cultures can be difficult to integrate. We at OfficeMax were street fighters with a relatively short history; Boise was an old-line company very much set in its ways. On a more positive note, after many years of hard work and some sacrifice, it is gratifying that the OfficeMax name was chosen as the go-forward combined corporate name.

So, what does my selling at the top really prove? The answer—as I have stated in other parts of this book—is that I would much rather be lucky than good.

However, when one is lucky (read that as being in the right place at the right time), one has to be smart enough to recognize the opportunity and go for it. And that's just what I did.

40

Lesson #40:
How to Put Lightning Back in the Bottle Again and Again— Many Entrepreneurs Are Serial Entrepreneurs

PICK UP THE paper, turn on the TV, or scan the Internet on any given day, and there's a good chance that you will learn about some superstar who is making a comeback—sometimes for the second or third time. Those who comprise this unique breed could be rock or movie stars, athletes or politicians, and, yes, even corporate entrepreneurs or executive whiz kids who have all but faded into the sunset and in many cases become yesterday's news.

The bigger question is this: Though they may have done it once, can these mere mortals do it again?

There are numerous theories about why former stars who have made their marks on the world would want to risk reputation, money, and self-esteem to grab for that elusive brass ring one more time. Second chances at fame and fortune often require defying Mother Nature and the aging process, which we all know can be dicey. Sports overachievers periodically seize the headlines with their resurrections. In the business world—which does not necessarily require as many physical attributes—the odds of a successful curtain call and standing ovation at the end of the day are somewhat improved over those for a super-jock. That is because mental dexterity is the required ingredient in commerce, rather than just sheer physical skills and endurance—although it does take a certain degree of strength to play in the show.

Company founders and CEOs, or a combination thereof, can more easily pull off a second hit by following a disciplined, straightforward process. It is not unheard of for an executive to do it right once and then repeat the success somewhere else. Within a year or two of a comeback attempt, the world knows if the business maestro did it or it was a flop. Talk about putting a spotlight on one's achievements or failures! It does not get any better or worse than this.

Some businesspeople do it for the money. Nevertheless, I would bet that most do it because they strongly believe they can, and are classic, calculating, risk-taking, type-A overachievers who want to show the world they aren't one-act wonders. I've found that the best executives, as with almost all others, always have something to prove to themselves or somebody close to them. This provides the encore performer a strong incentive to jump back into the fray.

One always makes mistakes while building anything. However, the biggest mistake is to repeat the previous error of omission or commission in a new undertaking. There are countless serial entrepreneurs who keep developing a growing string of successes. Each seems to have a common gene in their DNA that provides the ultimate high when they create/build a better mousetrap that fuels jobs, opportunities, and financial security for themselves as well as their employees, supporters, investors, and suppliers. The other common characteristic of serial achievers is that they need the bright lights, a stage, and a fair amount of control. Very few who make it more than once are gunslinger, shoot-from-the-hip types who come up with an idea and just follow their gut feelings; few of these can make it big twice. Instead, most successful second-act players have honed their instincts and skills and created a series of methodical steps that they follow, each of which keeps them off the rocks in the climb to the top. They understand the basics of how to get from A to Z while minimizing pain and wasted motions and maximizing available capital and talent. Past experience has taught them where to spend the most time and effort to ensure that they meet or beat both others' and their own expectations.

This reincarnation is not limited to just CEOs and entrepreneurs. It is also prevalent among supersalespeople and specialists of all sizes, shapes, and types.

There is a rhythm to success and a maze to navigate. However, if they have done it before, there is a better-than-even chance that they can put the lightning back in the bottle once more. The much-celebrated crooner Frank Sinatra summarized it well when he sang, "The best is yet to come."

So, after 15 years and 7 months, the curtain came down on my time at OfficeMax. At approximately noon on December 8, 2003, I unceremoniously left the company that I had built from scratch and drove about five miles to a vanilla (though upscale) industrial park in a Cleveland suburb to take up residence at a new private equity company that I was launching called Max-Ventures. Joining me in the new offices—which measured about 2,000 square feet, compared to the 200,000- square-foot Office-Max building that had been my sandbox until that day—were a secretary/administrative assistant who came with me from OfficeMax and my longtime investment banking friend who had helped me sell OfficeMax to Boise Cascade and who decided to leave McDonald & Company to partner with me.

The deal had netted me a princely sum of tens of millions of dollars, a good reputation as an entrepreneur, and thousands upon thousands of OfficeMax associates who thought that while I was running the company I was a reincarnation of Vince Lombardi—the famed Green Bay Packers football coach who had a reputation for being a hard-driving, disciplined winner (with an emphasis on the hard-driving component).

The lesson I learned quickly about reputations after I sold OfficeMax is that, like fine wines, they get better with just a little bit of aging. Many of my former associates, who perhaps thought I was unrelenting, soon began recounting stories about how things got done, how problems were solved, and how people made money on my watch.

Numerous people have asked me what I did to celebrate that day. Many thought I would jump on a private jet and fly off to some exotic venue with 100 of my closest friends and family. Others were sure I would throw the granddaddy of all parties that evening to commemorate what many would have considered a lifetime achievement.

However, I didn't do any of these things. For me it was simply a matter of getting into my car and driving the five miles to the new office, moving in, unpacking a few boxes, and then—as was my custom at OfficeMax—leaving for the day around 7:30 PM.

The next morning, I began Act II of my entrepreneurial life. I showed up at the new office with absolutely nothing to do other than to look at prospective deals and start to figure out how to manage my newfound wealth, which was a big job but not particularly exciting.

The big question that I had to quickly answer for myself was how I was going to remain relevant. Although I had the ability to use a laser focus to accomplish objectives, I also knew that I would bore easily and would need a full plate of tasks and projects to continue to flourish.

Some things changed instantly after the sale. Instead of having casts of literally hundreds to do whatever I needed, I had to revert back to lessons learned in previous lives about how to handle things for myself.

As a matter of full disclosure, however, I must point out that I had a five-year noncompete contract with OfficeMax/Boise, which in effect was a deal sweetener—or an extra piece to my golden parachute, as some would call it. The sweetener's provisions comprised a million-dollar-a-year salary, 100 percent free rent for my new offices, salary for my administrative assistant, and a continuation of having access to the latest and greatest gadgets with all the flashing lights and such. I had a number of other perks on top of all that, including accounting and legal consultation at no cost, security protection advice, and the usual trappings of a reigning CEO of a Fortune 500 company.

All of this was certainly nice, and I definitely did not have to worry about my next meal. However, I was concerned about continuing to make my mark. I have always believed that the successful entrepreneur is motivated by the need to "be in the game."

I began receiving a gazillion business plans and offers at my new company, virtually from the first day of operations. What astounded me most in reviewing these plans was how poorly entrepreneurs thought out their strategies and how so many really didn't have a clue as to what it would take to succeed. Indeed, one of the reasons I wrote this book is because there is a need for it. It quickly became apparent to me that helping others build their own businesses might not be for me. I was used to being at the epicenter of the action and having the power to act as the catalyst in driving results. Consulting, which I did for a bit in my new life, came naturally to me, but it also lacked fulfillment for me, as I would never be able to enjoy the sweet taste of victory. Instead, I would be that high-priced hired gun who came in to solve specific problems and then moved on, not knowing—or perhaps not even caring—about the story's final chapter.

It didn't take long for me to realize that I needed a new plan— one that was focused on a few things that had meat on their bones and where I could make a contribution. I also wanted to figure out a way to give something back to the community.

Within the first six months of Max-Ventures, I funded and raised money for a human resource psychological assessment firm designed to serve retailers as well as other businesses. I also joined some corporate boards and agreed to join numerous philanthropic boards of directors. And I made a few private equity investments in companies that I thought had some potential.

But there was still something missing.

A longtime friend of mine named Fred Koury—the founder of Smart Business Network and *Smart Business*, a successful chain of business magazines published in key markets coast-to-coast—suggested that I consider writing a guest column for the magazine. A lightbulb went off and I said to myself, "Author, author."

I prided myself on being an effective communicator over the course of my career and I particularly enjoyed communicating by using narrative prose. My first job had been as a copywriter at an advertising agency. Although the job was short-lived and not particularly lucrative, I had enjoyed it very much.

So I agreed to write the column, and after the first one came another and then another. Eventually, my column was being published monthly in all 17 *Smart Business* publications, as well as online. More astounding to me was that people were actually reading what I wrote—and I knew this because I began receiving fan mail almost from the first column. Business owners and CEOs, to whom the magazine is targeted, would write and say that my columns resonated with them, and although they never thought of it in the way I presented the theory, they got it now.

My columns quickly began taking on a life of their own. They became the subject of discussions at a number of business forums around the country, and also won a number of prestigious journalism awards. All of this led to receiving numerous invitations to speak.

At first, I was an easy mark. If an organization, school, or charity asked me to speak, I would do it—simply because it was the right thing to do. However, I also found myself accepting speaking engagements for businesses. And then it dawned on me: Why was I doing this for free?

Instead of agreeing simply to speak, my assistant would start fielding requests and then send a form letter and agreement stating that my speaking fee was between $10,000 and $25,000, depending on whether it was a for-profit enterprise or a business group with paying members. Interestingly enough, I found the more I charged, the more popular I became. In the process, I got very good at giving advice and quickly turned this advice business into an extremely lucrative operation. This became a good lesson in marketing and packaging.

Then, about three and a half years after selling OfficeMax, I started to think that it was time for my encore presentation. So when the opportunity for Max-Wellness came around, I was ready.

I recognize that most of us are what we are and we do what we do best. This means that although I now have a better balance in my life, I am still an entrepreneur, creator, builder, and doer at heart. I do not particularly enjoy being a philosopher or one who hypothesizes. The only exception to this is my writing and the column I produce like clockwork for *Smart Business* publications. Instead, I much prefer taking a blank piece of paper and turning it into a plan that can be implemented, then translating that plan into a living, breathing brand—a business that one can see, touch, and smell.

I also learned that although I made my mark as measured in creating wealth, I find the chase to be much more satisfying than the catch. The best and most enjoyable times in my life were probably during the first year or so of OfficeMax. I had no clue how difficult the task ahead would be, and had little idea about the intricacies of running a start-up business, let alone a Fortune 500 company, which OfficeMax would become in relatively short order.

What I really enjoy is doing it, instead of just telling others how to do it and then walking away. It probably goes back to the saying that those who can, do; those who can't, teach. Although I enjoy teaching, I prefer to be the guy carrying the ball, in the bright lights, on the stage, with the big audience and lots of control.

Some have called me a serial entrepreneur, although I have never considered myself an entrepreneur because, as far as I'm concerned, I am much too methodical and a little scared. Like many successful entrepreneurs and operators, I probably live to work rather than work to live. I love the challenge, thrive on naysayers telling me it can't be done, and get great satisfaction in proving the pessimists wrong. I won't presume to understand the psychological reason why anybody does anything, but the simple answer for me is that I put lightning back in the bottle because I know I can.

There's nothing more gratifying to me than starting from scratch and building a giant organization. There's nothing more fulfilling than providing people who join me along the way with the opportunity to have skin in the game and be in a unique situation to go further faster than they could go anyplace else.

I also know that although I truly love the limelight, I've learned in recent years that mentoring others is one of the most gratifying things one can do. To stare across the desk at a young manager and be able to point him or her in the right direction and then watch that person succeed—well, it doesn't get much more gratifying than that.

As I've written throughout this book, a business, product, or entrepreneurial life span happens in four distinct phases, and each one can be just as exciting as the others. You just have to recognize it while it's happening.

I never considered myself a huge risk taker. I would instead define my style as a cold, calculating opportunist, seizing the brass ring when I had a better-than-even chance of grabbing hold and holding on. And, during this second act of building the next OfficeMax in the form of Max-Wellness, I have actually found the experience much easier and more fulfilling.

There are obvious reasons.

First, much like a gunslinger, I've now developed a reputation that has served me well in recruiting a top-notch management team, raising equity money, and convincing landlords and vendors to extend a relatively large amount of credit to us when the balance sheet doesn't necessarily justify doing so. If entrepreneurs and executives focus on the journey as much as the ultimate destination, there's a decent chance that they can succeed. Anyone can be a flash-in-the-pan success; not many people have the sustainability to deliver month in and month out, year after year.

I'm a big believer in innovating, in never being satisfied with the status quo, and in finding new ways to do old things. I believe in hedging my bets, and when the time is right, pulling from the pot. Whenever given the opportunity, buy or build your company once and sell it as many times as you can. That's what OfficeMax became for me and my employees. Building once and selling three times changed many lives for the better, including my own.

One of the biggest faults of entrepreneurs is that they spend the majority of their time looking for the exit sign instead of watching for forks in the road. There is a general belief that one has to leave in order to cash out. To the contrary, there are many opportunities to pull money off the table and at the same time double down for the future. It gets down to having one's cake and eating it, too.

So, do I really think most entrepreneurs live to work or work to live? I think it depends on the place you are at in your life at any given point in time. The real answer is probably both. I really haven't decided what I want to do when I grow up, and with any luck I'll never grow up and will continue to have the ability to dream and convince others to join me on the journey.

Until then, I'll just have to be satisfied with thinking about how to move products, services, and companies through their life spans from mind to market, and then start over again. What goes around, definitely from my experience, comes around—again and again.

Epilogue

MORE QUESTIONS THAN answers—that's a good thing.

If you have read this far, I hope you enjoyed this road map for how I build businesses. It has certainly worked well for me. In many respects, this book could be considered a *Benevolent Dictator's Handbook*.

My main job both in building companies and in writing about doing so is that of Chief Pot Stirrer. I hope this book has made you think and provoked you to ask yourself key questions about what it will take for you to achieve what you've set out to do in your world.

An important question you should ponder when you turn the last page of this book is: To achieve your goals to create, build, and grow a company, do you have to—or want to—be a benevolent dictator?

I submit that it all depends on how you can best drive the process, and what style works best for you. One size never fits all. I have long realized that a start-up entrepreneur is always fighting the clock. Each tick represents a reduction in resources, both money and energy. As that incessant business clock ticks away, you often can't wait for colleagues to come around to your thinking. Therefore, it's up to you to pull the trigger on certain make-or-break moves. That doesn't mean operating in a vacuum. Instead, it requires learning how to weigh the input of all pertinent parties, analyzing the pros and cons—and then just doing it.

Will this style work for you? It really gets down to where you've been, what you've learned along the way, and where you want to go.

No matter where you want to end up, the best advice I have for you is this: Make the journey as exciting and fulfilling as the final destination.

And, never ever forget—capitalism rocks!

Index

THE
BENEVOLENT
DICTATOR

Now that you've read *The Benevolent Dictator*, your journey toward navigating your business to success has just begun. As part of your purchase, we've made available a variety of exclusive bonus features for you to access, download, and attend. Here are just a few of those items to help you take the next step toward achieving your entrepreneurial goals.

Visit **www.benevolentdictator.biz/resources**
to download these FREE resources:

Leadership & Readers Guide

Do you have what it takes to be a Benevolent Dictator and lead an organization through the four phases of its business lifespan? Download these special leadership and readers' guides and you'll be on your way. These two programs offer a series of questions for you to consider as you read this book as well as a roadmap for how to break down and implement the lessons within.

Special Webinar

It can be lonely at the top, despite the spectacular view. So where can you turn to get the answers you need to help you make decisions, as well as put yourself in the mindset of your peers? Join Benevolent Dictator Michael Feuer, editor/contributor Dustin S. Klein and a special CEO guest for a one-hour interactive Webinar where you'll not only get a chance to pose your questions to the author, but have an opportunity to hear ideas from another successful entrepreneur.

RESOURCES

How to grow your business in unusual places

There's no shortage of capital for those who know where to find it and how to secure it. In this exclusive audio podcast, Benevolent Dictator Michael Feuer pulls the curtain back and reveals what savvy entrepreneurs know about the unusual places you can find working capital to use to build – and grow – your company.

How to put lightning back in the bottle again and again

Entrepreneurship often is a lifestyle rather than a job. And that means encore performances. Unlike sports stars trying to regain lost glory, company founders and CEOs have a better chance of pulling off a second hit by following a disciplined, straightforward process that requires mental acumen rather than physical prowess. In this exclusive podcast, Benevolent Dictator Michael Feuer shares his secret sauce for making second, third, or even fourth entrepreneurial ventures successful.

→ Visit **www.benevolentdictator.biz/resources**
for your FREE resources.